Anonymous

Through North Wales With a Knapsack

Anonymous

Through North Wales With a Knapsack

ISBN/EAN: 9783744752763

Printed in Europe, USA, Canada, Australia, Japan

Cover: Foto ©Andreas Hilbeck / pixelio.de

More available books at **www.hansebooks.com**

THROUGH NORTH WALES

WITH A KNAPSACK

BY

FOUR SCHOOLMISTRESSES

"... though on pleasure she was bent,
She had a frugal mind"
Cowper

"Here's a plain unvarnished tale, and true to nature"

LONDON
KEGAN PAUL, TRENCH, TRÜBNER & CO., Ltd.
1890

INTRODUCTION.

I AM one of the four, and have been commissioned by the other three to write a few sentences of introduction to the following pages—our joint work.

The "summer holiday" is fast becoming a national institution, and is deservedly popular, for, besides affording a means of rest to weary workers, it offers possibilities of enjoyment in anticipation, realization, and recollection which no other recreation can rival. But, granted that a holiday of some kind during the summer months is both desirable and pleasant, it is not always easy to decide on its exact form, especially when time and means are limited. Last summer we four solved the question for ourselves by a Walking Tour, and our tour proved so pleasant, and has given rise to so many inquiries from our friends, that we are encouraged to think some account of our experiences may be of interest to a wider circle of holiday-seekers. We propose, therefore, in this little volume, to describe the incidents and course of our route, and to give an account of our equipment and expenditure.

When the Originator of the plan, an enterprising Newnham friend, asked me if I was inclined to join a walking-tour, my first impulse was to reply, "Impossible;" for I am a person of personal possessions, and the idea of spending twenty-one days with no more of these possessions than I could carry in a bag on my shoulders seemed at first insupportable. Some one has defined civilization as "the multiplication of essentials," and though this may be an imperfect and irreverent view of a great factor in the world's history, it contains some truth, and is easy to illustrate. When I reflect that many of my so-called "necessities" were luxuries to my mother, and unknown to my grandmother, I am ashamed; and when I think of the probable indispensables of the "young lady" a century hence, I shudder. The Originator controverted my arguments, and talked of classic simplicity and rural charms; but *I* studied the moderns at Newnham, and am town-bred, so such suggestions did not carry much weight. But the idea of discarding a little of our sham civilization and aids to happiness in the shape of bottles and mixtures grew more tempting with contemplation, and I enrolled myself as one of the party, and have never regretted my action.

INTRODUCTION.

The Originator suggested the idea to a near relation of her own—a disciple of art—and to a Girton graduate whose Alpine experiences and scientific skill proved most conducive to the success of our tour.

Our friends warned us against the expedition, and prophesied calamity, and were good enough to provide us with advice so varied in kind, that when we did start, we were prepared—so far as precept might avail—to meet any catastrophe travelling humanity can sustain.

Despite these difficulties, and many of a much more tangible nature, the Originator, who has the spirit of a born *entrepreneur*, triumphed. She studied maps and routes, gathered information from the few who were qualified to give it, soothed alarms, and conquered in detail each objection as it arose.

Advice as to our equipment we received till our brains whirled. Opinions as regards quantity varied from a complete change of garments, including a hat and dress, down to a brown-paper parcel containing a night-dress and tooth-brush! As a matter of fact, our luggage was simple enough. In the matter of dress individual taste must be consulted, but we strongly recommend a substantial underskirt, simple dress-skirt capable of being tucked up at need, a jersey bodice and extra blouse, and a broad-brimmed hat. Do not, however, trim the hat with flowers. Mine started adorned with poppies, now, alas! scattered through North Wales by the four winds of heaven. A jacket or shawl is absolutely necessary; caps we found useful for climbing. We carried mackintoshes with us, but they are most difficult to wear with a pack, and in future I shall adopt a dress-skirt of waterproof material, and trust to a jacket for further protection against bad weather. Umbrellas we found most serviceable, but perhaps in a dry season sticks would do as well. A small basket and a bag to hold our luncheon and botanical spoil completed our luggage.

The special advantages of a walking tour are so obvious that I need not expatiate upon them. Every pedestrian knows something of the pleasure of surveying beautiful scenery at leisure, trying new roads and short cuts, and pausing at will to examine a rare flower or bush. To these joys a walking tour adds the crowning bliss of constant progress onwards. The miles of dusty road or grassy sward, as the case may be, need not be retraced; at every step new possibilities open out before the traveller, and the dinner-bell has lost its power.

Nor need any one be deterred from tasting these pleasures by the idea that unusual physical strength is necessary to obtain them. We were people of very average capacity, and if one of us is perhaps stronger than falls to the lot of most of the race, I, on the other hand, pass for rather a weakly individual, and yet I can confidently affirm that, with the exception of one day when the rain made walking a toil, I never sustained exceptional fatigue.

But—and this I would emphasize most strongly—we did not walk for the sake of making a fine record in miles, nor did we hesitate to have a lazy day when we felt inclined for it.

Bearing this in mind, and starting with a fair stock of patience, good temper, and enterprise, I feel sure that ladies may easily and safely achieve an average of ten or twelve miles a day, and in so doing secure an extremely profitable and pleasant holiday.

In conclusion, I may say that we shall be pleased to give any further information in our power to any correspondent who may care to write to us under cover of our publishers.

CONTENTS.

CHAPTER		PAGE
I.	BIRMINGHAM TO TREFRIW	1
II.	TREFRIW	4
III.	TREFRIW (*Continued*)	9
IV.	TREFRIW TO BETTWS-Y-COED	13
V.	BETTWS-Y-COED TO LLYN OGWEN VIÂ CAPEL CURIG	19
VI.	LLYN OGWEN TO LLANBERIS	28
VII.	LLANBERIS	37
VIII.	LLANBERIS TO BEDDGELERT VIÂ PEN-Y-GWRYD	42
IX.	BEDDGELERT	50
X.	BEDDGELERT (*Continued*)	53
XI.	BEDDGELERT TO PENRHYN-DEUDRAETH AND SNOWDON	57
XII.	PENRHYN TO DOLGELLY VIÂ FESTINIOG AND THE MOUNT MORGAN GOLD MINE	67
XIII.	DOLGELLY	82
XIV.	DOLGELLY TO BARMOUTH VIÂ CADER IDRIS AND ARTHOG	84
XV.	BARMOUTH TO LLANUWCHYLLYN	89
XVI.	LLANUWCHYLLYN	93
XVII.	LLANUWCHYLLYN TO CORWEN	95
XVIII.	CORWEN TO BIRMINGHAM	101
XIX.	SUPPLEMENTARY	105

Beaumaris

MENAI STRAIT

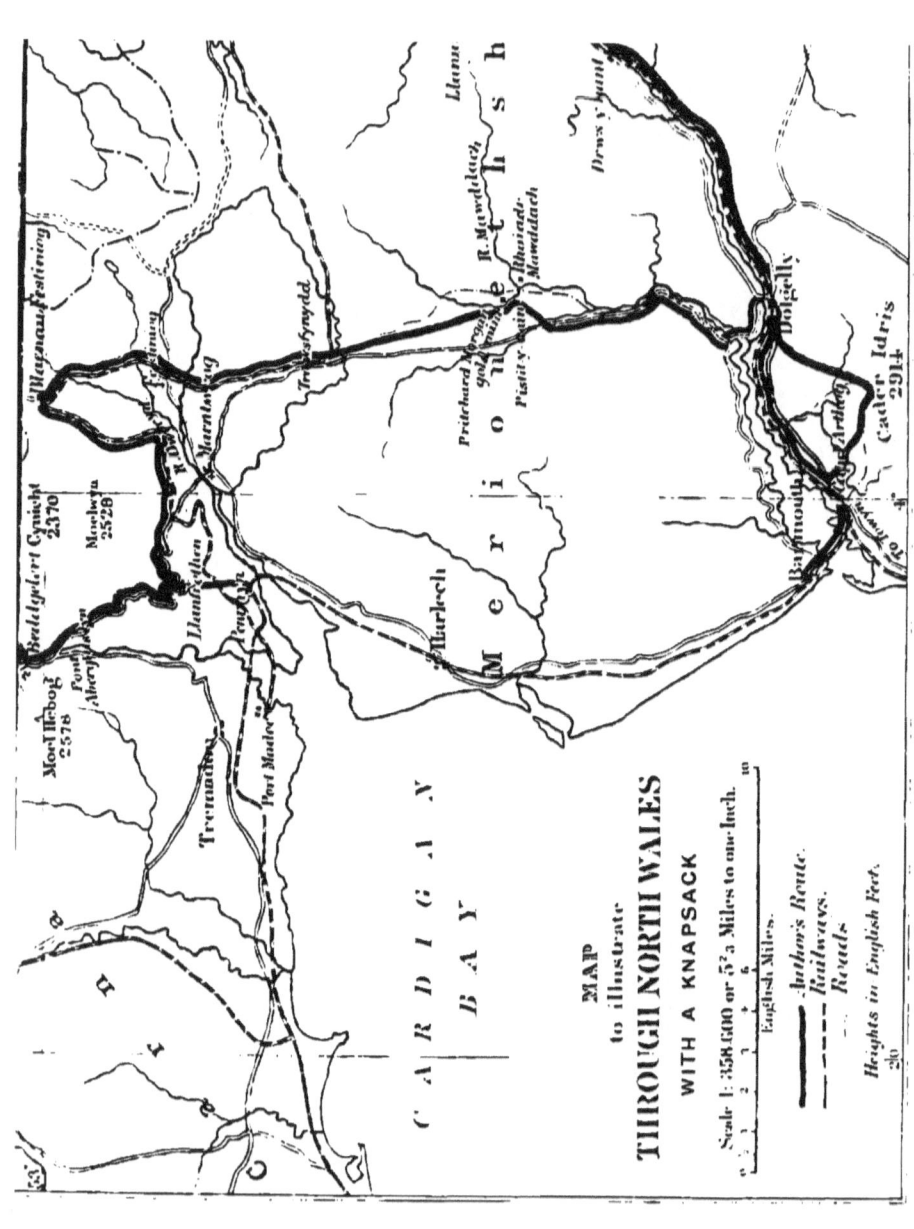

THROUGH NORTH WALES
WITH A KNAPSACK.

CHAPTER I.

BIRMINGHAM TO TREFRIW.

Saturday, August 4, 1888.—We left Birmingham early in the afternoon, and were accompanied to the station and "seen off" by a large band of friends, who gave us many final scraps of advice, and evidently regarded us so much in the light of pioneers, that we began to think we really were engaging in a perilous enterprise.

Railway journeys are apt to be prosaic, and ours proved no exception. We had taken third-class excursion tickets for economy's sake, and were a little surprised at the very pleasant company we had all the way. At Colwyn Bay we were greeted by friends; and at Llandudno Junction we finally broke the monotony by leaving the train, and, finding we had some two hours to wait before we could proceed, decided to walk into Conway and look for tea. Drenching rain prevented our exploring the town, and, after getting some food in a quaint old inn parlour, and taking note of Telford's suspension bridge and the old castle walls, we were glad to return to the railway station in good time to catch the 8.15 train for Llanrwst, eleven miles up the Conway valley, and the station for Trefriw.

As we neared our destination, we began to adjust our knapsacks, which we expected to carry in correct pedestrian fashion from Llanrwst Station; but the evident surprise and horror of one of our fellow-travellers, a clergyman, compelled us to delay operations, and when we arrived at the station, we found a waggonette ready to carry ourselves and our packs to the lodgings we had already engaged.

We were not sorry for this piece of foresight on the part of our hostess, as the rain would have made a walk in the dusk very unpleasant; as it was, we reached our lodgings in rather a damp and draggled condition, with more than one rent in our mackintoshes, and Constance reported her umbrella invalided.

Our rooms were most satisfactory, the parlour especially being designed to suit all tastes, as it was decorated with portraits of John Bunyan, Lord Beaconsfield and Gladstone, and a group of Salvation "lasses" who had recently stayed here, and pleased the hostess by being such "good-living people." There were also two good landscapes in oils, left by an artist, a former lodger. We examined the various works of art, did a little unpacking, rejoicing that we had *so* little to do, and after supper were glad to go to bed.

CHAPTER II.

TREFRIW.

Sunday, August 5.—A very lovely, breezy morning, with a look of fine weather. Margery, Christina, and Constance started to explore before breakfast, leaving Leonora (whose laziness on this occasion has labelled her for the time with the title of "the sluggard") still sleeping off the fatigue of the journey. The valley is wide, with meadows on each side of the Conway, sloping up to well-wooded hills—everything very green this season. The houses are of stone, bare or plastered, many whitewashed, and all with slate roofs. The roads and paths are made of crumbled slate, and the stones in the little churchyard, on which our rooms looked, are of slate too, and curiously thin.

Near by is a deep glen, with a lovely series of waterfalls, the water passing over many ledges of rock, with deep hollows and pot-holes, and crossed by light bridges and overhung with trees. The stream turns several mill-wheels, all quiet on Sunday—as was, indeed, the whole village.

The explorers brought back a bonny nosegay of harebells, yellow nipplewort, St. John's wort, pennywort, foxgloves, meadow-sweet, crane's-bill, grasses, and various ferns—male fern, lady fern, lastrea, and splendid polypodies.

A Welsh service was held in the church about ten, and immediately afterwards an English one, which we attended. We noticed here, and subsequently in other places, that while the *churchyard* inscriptions were all in Welsh, those on tablets *inside* the church were in English. This is paralleled by the custom, formerly so common in England, of placing Latin inscriptions in the holy building, while those without were in the common tongue.

As there was no second English service, we devoted the afternoon, and as much of the evening as was necessary, to exploring the neighbourhood.

We started, after an early dinner, by a good wide path along the glen to Llyn (Lake) Crafnant, rising steadily, but slowly, and crossing many tributaries of the brook which comes down from Crafnant, and forms the Fairy Falls at Trefriw.

Margery and Christina had plenty of chances of gratifying their botanical taste, and were delighted to find quantities of bell-heather, bog-myrtle, and cotton-grass; while Constance and Leonora were equally charmed to come across real "fields of asphodel," which afforded scope for any amount of quoting.

After a good two miles, we crossed the stream near a fine fall, and soon reached Llyn Crafnant, a shimmering sheet of water surrounded by hills. Leaving the lake to the left, we struck up the hillside, where, after a good scramble through grass and heather (quite dry, in spite of recent rain), we camped and refreshed ourselves—physically with chocolate and biscuits, and mentally with a good look at the lake below and the hills around. After a rest, all too brief in the opinion of Leonora, who is an inveterate lounger, we continued the ascent, up some steep and slippery slopes, to the very top of the hill, from which a splendid view presented itself. North and east were heights, south and west wide valleys, with hills again beyond, and we counted no less than nine lakes, mostly in the direction of Capel Curig.

We made our way slowly down the steep southern face of the mountain, zigzagging a good deal, and stopping now and again to gather heather, finding *white* varieties of the three sorts, ling, bell, and five-leaved, and luscious strawberries growing on the tiniest plants among the rocks. Presently we reached an unpromising-looking stone wall, which we, however, easily crossed by following in the track of an active sheep, who unwittingly directed us to a ladder.

Having noted some fine *roches moutonnées*, we crossed the Geirionydd, near the pretty little lake of that name, but missed the monument to Taliesin, a bard who used to frequent these parts. Following a good path, hedged by splendid red wild roses, up the further side of the valley, we reached the church of Llanrwchwyn, the oldest, it is said, in Wales, and a very gruesome edifice indeed. The lych-gate, a solid door, whose lintel bore an inscription, "it : id : ot : 1462 : wo," was padlocked, but a woman appeared with the key, and showed us the church, a privilege which we shared with a party of young Welshmen, who arrived just as we did. From their questions and our own, we gathered that the woodwork of the church, including a rather fine roof, was put together without *iron*, only wooden pegs being used. The jambs of the door had been all of wood, and it turned on pivots, one of which had been replaced by iron. There were two aisles of the same size, divided by solid square pillars; the floor was of slate—very cold looking, open seats, no chancel, but a step *down* led to the altar rails, under one of the two windows, which were certainly not *east* by the sun. Fastened to the communion-rail is a curious, shallow, oblong wooden tray, into which are put the offerings made to the clergyman at a funeral. The clerk receives his in a wooden article not unlike a flat soup-ladle. There is a little very old stained glass in the windows, and in one we made out the words "orate p.," indicating that the inscription dates from pre-Reformation times. We found that, although Llanrhychwyn is the parish church, its doors are closed on Sunday, "because most of the people go to chapel;" but there is a service on Tuesday, which some of them attend.

Leaving the church, a little saddened by its chill, unused atmosphere, we went back to Trefriw through meadows, and a woody path densely covered with dead leaves.

The first day of our holiday was over, and had proved even more refreshing and pleasant than we had anticipated, and our anticipations were not modest!

CHAPTER III.

TREFRIW (*Continued*).

Monday, August 6.—The morning proved dull and rainy, so we spent the early hours indoors, Christina and Constance reading and writing, Leonora idling, and Margery sketching the view of the church from the window. The church is said to have been built by a certain Llewellyn to save his wife the trouble of going so far as Llanrychwyn Church, which he had built also; but, unfortunately, certain obvious architectural differences between the two buildings destroy the credibility of the little story, which must be relegated to the land of legend.

About noon the weather cleared, and we started for Cefn Careadwydd, a hill lying between Trefriw and Llyn Cowlyd. We found the path good, but steep, and very wet—economical, in fact, for a stream frequently shared the roadway with us. A rocky bank supplied us with heather, stonecrop, gorse, mosses, lichens, and ferns, and after a while we were able to regale ourselves with raspberries, and later with bilberries. The road grew steeper, wetter, and windier, and Leonora congratulated herself on having exchanged her broad straw hat for a close cap, though the broad hats had their uses in serving occasionally as umbrellas. We sheltered near a ruined cottage, half covered with polypodies and stonecrop, close by a bank studded with the delicate ivy-leaved blue campanula, while all round were great tufts of lady ferns, with elder bushes still in bloom; and beyond we had fine views over the Conway valley, and Llyns Geirionydd and Crafnant, and Taliesin's monument, which we had unaccountably missed in yesterday's expedition. Misty rain came on before we reached the top, and the heavy walking so fatigued Leonora, that she was left sitting on a stone, a disconsolate wet heap, while the rest of us pushed on and were rewarded by a sight of the Great Orme's Head, Moel Eilio, and Clogwyn Eira, though the peaks on the Snowdon side were lost in the mist which was rolling about, and warning us to descend. On the way down we picked up Leonora, who cheered up at the idea of descent and dinner, and we made our way down in forty minutes, having been out about two hours. We thought it prudent not to attempt another expedition without a good rest, being well convinced of the value of a motto suggested by a cautious friend, "slow and sure."

After five-o'clock tea, we started for Dolgarrog Falls, made by the stream which leaves Llyn Cowlyd, and comes over the heights to join the Conway. The road lies between the river and the wooded slopes on which Trefriw is built, and passes a famous chalybeate spring. It drizzled nearly all the way, but we were prepared for bad weather and did not mind, though the air was certainly very soft! After walking two miles and a half, we left the road, and climbed up to the falls, partly by a very wet red path (betraying the presence of iron), partly through the woods over grey boulders and beds of moss, in which were jewels of fungi, orange, amethyst, and crimson. We followed the falls till we reached the upper leap, a sheet of white water, drawn into thinnest threads, and dashing into a dark pool, to plunge on and on over huge rocks to the valley below.

There is another fall, Porth-lwyd, a mile further on, but we had no time to visit it, for it was nearly 8 p.m. before we began our rather slippery descent to the road.

We were much struck with the extreme loneliness of our walks. On Sunday we had hardly been surprised to meet only one hare, one squirrel, and three tourists; but on Monday, bank holiday too, we were certainly astonished to encounter only a couple of haymakers and another man on the road, though there were parties of people in the village itself. The falls had not been visited all day, so far as we could tell from the absence of footmarks, which would probably have been plainly visible on the damp earth.

Home we went, fairly weary after our ten or eleven miles.

Both on Sunday evening and Monday afternoon, the village resounded with fine singing, consisting of hymns and classical music, performed, as we understood, by a choir of Welsh visitors. They stood outside the churchyard, with "lanterns dimly burning," and poured forth their melody for at least two hours on Sunday, and nearly as long on Monday. Perhaps they were practising for the Eisteddfodd soon to be held at Wrexham; anyhow, the effect in the quiet village in the still evening was extremely good.

CHAPTER IV.

TREFRIW TO BETTWS-Y-COED.

Tuesday, August 7.—A most glorious morning greeted us, golden sunshine everywhere. We were glad of the favourable weather, for when, after breakfasting, packing, and settling our very moderate bill, we shouldered our knapsacks and set off through the wood, we were homeless wanderers in good earnest, and had no definite plan beyond that of reaching Bettws-y-coed before nightfall. We started by way of Llyn-y-parc, the road being a steady ascent, through woods and over moorland. We had not walked far before sounds of distress were heard from Leonora and Constance, who found their knapsacks unbearable. Explanation was easy—Leonora had *crossed* the straps on her chest, which made breathing a matter of difficulty; while Constance had belted one strap tightly round her waist, and found that plan equally uncomfortable. The remedy was not so easily found, but, after various alterations and alleviations, and a little grumbling, we hit on the right plan, which is to form loops of the two knapsack straps, and pass an arm through each loop. Worn in this way, we never felt the slightest discomfort in carrying our packs, and, indeed, before long we grew so much accustomed to them, that Christina was suspected of a desire to wear hers constantly; it was "like carrying an armchair," she said, "so immensely convenient for leaning against stone walls and surveying the landscape at ease."

We passed one pretty waterfall, and many streamlets made music as we went. A long pull up a pretty but very steep road, close to some lead mines, which are doing their best to spoil the face of nature, brought us to the edge of the park, or rather forest, in which is the Llyn, about half a mile long, with deep indigo blue waters, surrounded on three sides by woods, and on the fourth by fine grey rocks, sprinkled with purple heather, the edge of barren hills.

We halted before leaving the lake, and asked the way of a ragged urchin, who appeared from a whitewalled, slate-roofed cottage hard by. He showed a strong desire to earn an honest penny, asked to be taken on as guide, and vouchsafed no unpaid information beyond warning us of many dangers in the path we had to take. But we dispensed with his services, and pursued our way to a lovely little glen, down which the lake stream rushes into the Conway below. On the right the glen was wooded, while the left was steep and craggy, with quantities of heather. We made our way down the wooded side—cautiously, for the boy was right in describing the path as narrow and rough, and our packs had to be balanced—past some deserted mines, which somewhat destroyed the beauty of the glen, until the road turned aside through the woods. There were many tracks, but we had taken our bearings correctly, and emerged at last in a little glade, opening on to some fields and a garden. Here we halted to eat the luncheon of sandwiches and biscuits we had brought from Trefriw, supplementing these provisions by some water Margery and Constance fetched from the cottage, a journey not accomplished without difficulty, for on the way they had to lower themselves into the cottage garden from one rocky terrace to another, and, returning, scramble up as best they might.

Meanwhile Christina and Leonora made their packs into pillows, and luxuriously reposed on the soft moss, though the luxury in Christina's case was more apparent than real, for when she left her turfy couch, she discovered that she had inadvertently been occupying a water-bed! We gave her a good deal of laughing sympathy, which she accepted thankfully for what it was worth, being one of those invaluable people who accept the worst of things in the best of tempers.

After our nooning, we donned our packs again, and went off through the woods to Bettws. Presently we had a distant prospect of a young lady, all beautiful in a blue cambric gown; so, realizing that we were nearing civilization, we untucked our skirts, and generally made a hasty toilet before asking directions for reaching the Miners' Bridge. This is a sort of ladder with rails, spanning a roaring torrent, clear brown water, foaming over or between pale grey rocks, worn into strange shapes, overhung with rowans full of berries and other trees reflected in the pools. "The most pleasant memory of our tour" is Leonora's verdict on the Miners' Bridge. We crossed the bridge, took a last reluctant gaze, and tramped along the main road to Bettws-y-coed to find lodgings.

Later, after more experience of friendly Welsh hospitality, and the facility of obtaining comfortable rooms for so short a time as one night, we did not hurry in our selection; but Bettws was the scene of our earliest lodging-hunt, and we accepted the first rooms that offered with more faith than sagacity. We offer these pages as a true account of our travels, and mean faithfully to record the "downs" as well as the "ups;" but there is no need to expatiate on the few discomforts we suffered, so it shall suffice to say that those rooms at Bettws were not a successful venture, and that we do *not* intend to recommend them to our friends. Afterwards, our arrangements for spending the night were left to Margery, whose inches gave her a stateliness which we found of value in more than one commercial transaction.

After tea and a rest, which Leonora preferred to prolong indefinitely, Margery, Christina, and Constance started for the Fairy Glen, one of *the* sights of North Wales.

We three passed the Beavers' Bridge, which crosses the Llugwy Falls, and the church, so well known from David Cox's sketches, though the view he so much loved has been damaged by the erection of a large railway station, whose presence we much regret, though doubtless it has its uses. We found the Fairy Glen to be a wooded, rocky gorge, through which the Conway rushes. The foliage here, as everywhere, was luxuriant in quantity, and exquisitely coloured, the vigorous midsummer shoot giving the appearance of early autumn in some places.

After admiring the glen, we proceeded to the old road, now become a grassy track, very pleasant to weary feet. Here the clouds, which had been hanging over the heights for some hours, gave us a regular drizzle, in spite of which we pushed on another two and a half miles, which brought us to the famous falls of the Conway. The water, which is like well-made coffee, and evidently comes through peat bogs, is broken into two foaming sheets by a large rock, on which is a salmon-ladder, dry and partly overgrown with ash trees. We left the falls with the impression that, though they are fine and their surroundings grand, Dolgarrog, for a fall, is far finer.

We returned to Bettws by Telford's wide and well-kept road, for which we were sincerely grateful, and also for the milestones, one of which prevented us from taking a wrong turning and going to Llanrwst!

In our absence, Leonora had made a raid on the station and secured a newspaper, our first since we left home; so we spent what was left of the evening in acquainting ourselves with the doings of the outside world.

CHAPTER V.

BETTWS-Y-COED TO LLYN OGWEN VIÂ CAPEL CURIG.

Wednesday, *August* 8.—Misty rain prevented our making an early start, but by nine o'clock we were *en route* for Capel. We followed the Telford road again, turning off about a mile from Bettws to see the well-known "Swallow Falls," or Rhaiadr-y-Wennol, where the Llugwy comes down to the valley in several splendid, broad, tumbling leaps.

The road to the falls and the actual descent was thronged with tourists, dressed for the most part in ulsters and cloth caps, so that it was difficult to tell from a distance whether the groups of people crowding on the slippery rocks were composed of men or women. We made our way down with the rest, and thoroughly enjoyed the sight of the foamy water, and the *feel* of the spray on our faces.

Satisfied at last, we returned to the high-road, noting with pleasure that we had done our first mile in fifteen minutes, an achievement we did not repeat that day, or on many other days. We often wondered if the Welsh mile is longer than its English brother.

The day grew warmer, and the sky gradually cleared, but the clouds hung persistently over Siabod and the Snowdon heights. The road was perfect all the way, and we were much amused to see a whole family of children on cycles, travelling in quite a unique fashion. A small Coventry led, then an ordinary tricycle, followed by a hill-climber, and finally a mail-cart, all linked together, and ridden by a girl of about thirteen, two boys, some sizes smaller, with a tiny girl and boy in the mail-cart.

On arriving at Capel Curig, we inquired at the post-office for letters and lodgings, and found plenty of the former article, but were told that the latter was not to be had, the village being full of anglers. So we adjourned to a comfortable wall at a little distance, to eat our luncheon and decide on our course of procedure.

Motives of economy compelled us to avoid large hotels, so there seemed nothing to do but push on along the Bangor road, and seek shelter at Ogwen (where we had already written to ask the extent of accommodation available), or, if necessary, further still, at Bethesda. Our choice was largely influenced by the fact that the Ogwen Valley basked in the sunshine, while the Snowdon side was hidden in drizzling mist. We never regretted our "weather-wise" decision.

Before starting, it was necessary to give some directions at the post-office, and to replenish our provision-bag; so we turned back into the village, and were there regarded with the most absolute and blatant curiosity and surprise by a little party of visitors. Before the end of our tour we were well accustomed to affording gratuitous amusement, and sometimes well amused in our turn, as Leonora and Constance usually walked a few paces behind Margery and Christina, and so were able to hear the comments educed by the appearance of these latter; but we all agreed that the undisguised astonishment of our Capel Curig inspectors was unequalled in all our travels.

Soon after turning our backs on Capel, we noticed a change in the landscape. Hitherto it had presented what is known as "a sunny appearance," but now the country grew more and more barren and wild at every step. On either hand were rock-strewn pastures, or peaty bogs, sloping up to desolate hills, Cefn-y-Capel, Galt-y-Gogo and Tryfan, round which the great clouds played, swirling and changing in shape and colour. The road stretched on, mile after mile, the sameness enlivened here and there by a grey cottage or a group of haymakers, and brightened by the sunshine, which made walking warm work, and rendered a rest by the roadside very agreeable, and gave Margery an opportunity of drying her cloak, which had not recovered from yesterday evening's walk in the rain. While she was engaged in turning a highly respectable stone wall into an amateur drying-ground, the rest of the party " shuffled off their mortal coils " (*i.e.* knapsacks), and ate chocolate in lieu of afternoon tea, all of which proceedings considerably astonished the passengers on the Bangor coach, which passed while we were still sitting by the roadside.

About five miles from Capel Curig we saw the last of the Llugwy, and the first of Llyn Ogwen, lying in the midst of rugged hills, Carnedd Dafydd, Y-Garn, Foel Goch, and Tryfan, the latter being composed of bare uptilted rock nearly from summit to base, with streams dashing down the " cwms " on either side, and two curious upright stones, like people, standing on the very peak.

In rounding the lake in search of the Cottage, where we hoped to find accommodation for the night, we saw several fishing-boats on the water, and presently came upon a picnic-party having tea, and looking remarkably jovial and fashionable, and not a little out of place amidst such severe scenery. When the Cottage came in sight, we were a little disturbed to discover that it certainly could not accommodate *many* people, and our misgivings increased when we realized that we were being rapidly overtaken by a coach, which might deposit some of its load at the cottage; but to our great relief the coach rolled on along the Bangor road without a pause.

We had written to Ogwen to inquire for rooms, but our "forced march" from Capel had not allowed time for an answer, so we made ourselves known, and asked for a reply in person. We found the kindly hostess, Mrs. Williams, at the door of the Cottage, whose kitchen furnished a background of shiny pots and pans, she wearing—according to the universal fashion in these parts—a man's hat over her cap. Bonnets are things unknown in the Principality, we suppose. The Cottage was full! A dialogue between Margery and Mrs. W., Margery pathetic: "We have come so far—are *so* anxious to see more of Ogwen—so unwilling to go on to Bethesda—have no luggage but our knapsacks—will sleep on anything; if necessary, a bundle of hay."

Mrs. Williams, at first stony: "Very sorry, miss, but quite full," repeated again and again. But she was not proof against the bundle of hay, backed by the mute pleading of the other three, who stood by, living examples of

> "Persuasive looks, and more persuasive sighs,
> Silence that speaks, and eloquence of eyes."

First she consented to take in two of us; but, being assured that separation was out of the question, she kindly promised to do her best; and finally took us into a large pleasant tea or luncheon room, where we sat down while some coffee was prepared.

We beguiled the time by reading a stray Baedeker (to whose owner we beg to tender our best thanks), and in watching the departure of the picnic-party. We gathered that this included a certain noble lord, rich in quarries, and his family; so, on hearing the murmur "Here comes Lord ——," some of us looked with considerable interest, to see—a regular tatterdemalion pass the window. The noble lord we never saw.

After coffee we set off for Llyn Idwal, famous in legend and song as the place where Prince Idwal, son of Owain Gwynedd, was murdered, and more remotely known as a place haunted by demons and shunned by birds.

We started just behind the Cottage and a little honemill, and looked for a path. As usual, it was a case of "water, water everywhere," so we followed a stream which did duty as a road, and in about twenty minutes found ourselves on the gloomy shores of Lake Idwal, untenanted save by some anglers in a boat.

Otherwise the place was quite solitary. Large crags of slaty rock, streaked with veins of pure white quartz, rise in a semicircle, over which tower Tryfan to the left, Foel Goch and Y-Garn to the right, looking up the lake, while great boulders at the foot of the crags lead up to a perilous chasm called "Twll Du," the Black Hole, or Devil's Kitchen.

We skirted the lake over stony green slopes, the remains of ancient moraines or rubbish heaps, brought down by the glacier which scooped out the lake in prehistoric ages. We had been told that in this desolate spot various rare ferns and some Alpine flowers had escaped the destructive hands of fern-hawkers, so we climbed among the boulders in the direction of Twll Du in search of rarities.

Presently Leonora and Constance proclaimed themselves "aweary of the quest," and sat down to take a somewhat dubious rest on the hard rock, and an equally dubious sketch of the "Kitchen." Margery and Christina pushed on, and in the course of a hard scramble were rewarded by finding specimens of filmy, oak, parsley, and beech ferns, as well as a rare saxifrage, the mountain sorrel, and splendid mosses.

Laden with treasure trove, we returned to the Cottage, following a sheep-track part of the way, and noticing that the Welsh sheep, besides being long-tailed, horned, and capital eating, are also extremely sagacious in their choice of paths, as they always select the driest places.

The track led us to a difficult wall, which called forth all our activity and courage; but, having surmounted it, we were delighted to find ourselves close to some *roches moutonnées* rounded by ancient glacier ice, and looking like elephants lying down in the rich green turf, with only their long grey backs visible.

We climbed the highest of these, and stayed on the top as long as the strong cool breeze would allow, and thence had a grand view.

Behind us—south—was the rocky wall above Idwal, and the heights of Tryfan, tipped with golden light in the setting sun. Before us was Braich-du, a grey triangular mass, from below which came up the roar of the Falls of Benglog, by which the Ogwen river leaves the lake and plunges down into the green, peaty valley of Nant Francon, through which it winds to Bangor and the sea. To the left of the valley, the mountains ended in the terraces of the Penrhyn slate quarries, and we could see the smoke of Bethesda, a large mining village, rising into the air; and beyond, again, a pale grey streak indicated the Menai Straits.

To our right lay the blue waters of Llyn Ogwen, with the heights of Carnedd Llewellyn and Penllithrig-y-Wrach, behind which, though invisible to us, were our old friends, Llyns Crafnant and Geirionydd.

Altogether this was one of the finest views we

remember, short of actual snowfields, and the absolute stillness and solitude added not a little to its charm.

We found supper waiting for us, and having done ample justice to the ham and eggs, we were ready for bed, having first examined the visitors' book, which is noteworthy in possessing a frontispiece by H. Herkomer. This, however, is not kept on the public table, for the book suffered so much at the hands of unprincipled visitors, that the hostess has deemed it prudent to take the contribution of the famous artist into her personal care.

CHAPTER VI.

LLYN OGWEN TO LLANBERIS.

Thursday, August 9.—We had planned an early start, but, though our vows were not "made in wine," they were none the less broken, and the sun was high in the heavens before we met at breakfast. Margery and Constance explained that they would have been ready sooner had not the limited area of their room rendered hair-brushing a feat of some difficulty, and their efforts to obtain more space had resulted in the intrusion of a large collie! Moreover, they had already enjoyed the morning air by the shore of the lake, blue and glittering in the sun. Christina had slept late rather than early, owing to the charms of the moonlight on the water, together with physical fears connected with the possible collapse of her bed —a kind of wardrobe, most attractive to sleep in while it remained a bed, but apparently liable to become a wardrobe again at a moment's notice. As for Leonora, she proclaimed herself alike indifferent to moon and sun, but keenly interested in the breakfast. She had watched our hostess preparing it in the exquisitely neat kitchen, where everything that could shine, shone. The meal over, we packed, mutually strapped on our knapsacks, deciding as we did so that our appearance vividly recalled a certain picture in the year's Academy, "The Burden of Many Years."

After obtaining directions as to the best route to Llanberis from the neighbouring hone-miller, Mrs. Williams serving as interpreter, and taking a regretful farewell of Llyn Ogwen, we started over the mountains.

At first we followed an old, almost disused road, but soon left the track and proceeded up the slopes, making for a little "cwm," or hollow, between Y-Garn and Foel Goch.

We soon found cause to regret our tardy departure from the Cottage, for our way lay wholly in the sun, and the rocky pastures, though gay with saxifrages and red with sundews, were also sufficiently steep to make climbing hard work and botanical explorations less attractive than usual.

Leonora was soon heard—considerably in the rear—delivering a lecture on the "Luxury of Lounging," and the folly of measuring pleasure by miles; and, this logic appearing unanswerable in the hot August sunshine, we decided on making frequent halts, and not hastening our arrival at Llanberis.

After a while, our track was crossed by a very high and shaky-looking wall, which threatened to be a serious obstacle to our progress. Search brought us to a point where a huge flat rock formed a platform on our side, but there was a bog on the other, and bogs, we had discovered by experience, are not pleasant to land in after a jump. We sent over a few flat stones from the top of the wall, followed by Christina, who found firm footing for herself, and encouraged Margery and Constance to follow her example, Leonora and the packs making the venture last.

By noon we fairly reached the little cwm, and found a pleasant camping-ground on a rock in the midst of what had been, and is still called in the Ordnance Map, "Llyn Cywion," but the lake-bed is now a peat bog, with a few pools of brown water here and there.

A lovely clear stream supplied us with water to fill our tin saucepan, and, having lighted our "etna," we soon prepared a "billy" of tea, which, mixed with cold water, we found most refreshing. We do not mean that a little strong tea diluted with cold water is preferable to the ordinary beverage, but that the former makes a good substitute for the latter when milk-jugs and tea-pots are not at hand.

Together with the tea we discussed some Capel Curig buns, which proved too substantial even for our mountain appetites, and, after trying them in various fashions—dipped in water, in tea, with a biscuit—we abandoned several for the use of the sheep.

So far the weather had been glorious, but mists continued to rise from Nant-Francon and girdle Braich-du, white clouds flecked the blue sky, and the veering wind—from south-east to south, and then south-west—all denoted change, and warned us not to tarry.

To get out of the bog was fairly easy, as Margery had reconnoitred ahead, and we made for some smooth scraped rocks, some of them scored by ice. Then came a long clamber over large blocks of stone, among which, and in the "screes" of slippery slates on a slope which succeeded the boulders, grew magnificent tufts of parsley fern, untouched as yet by fern-hunters. Christina could not resist the ferns, and filled her handkerchief with roots, thereby adding to her responsibilities in a manner we by no means approved.

Now came the crux of the whole day, and, indeed, of the entire tour. To quit the cwm, bounded on three sides by a high steep ridge, we had to choose between a long slope of slippery-looking turf, stretching up in the hot sun, with few projecting points to give foothold, and rocks with boggy turf, lying more in shadow, and with plenty of points, though they did not look exactly friendly.

We started together, but Leonora, who held that safety lay in speed, went in advance, and after many disappointments as to arrival at the summit, and a few difficult bits of climbing, reached the top in triumph, and had her reward in the amusement of seeing the rest arrive, hot, weary, and not a little dishevelled.

The turf was wet, and sometimes we had to crawl, getting hands, feet, and knees very damp; but the real trouble lay in managing our umbrellas and packs, which threatened to overbalance at times. Margery was additionally laden with the provision-basket, and she and Constance both felt anxious about Christina, whose progress was growing more and more uncertain and unsteady, though she refused to abandon the bundle of ferns. However, steadiness of purpose seemed to do as well as steadiness of head, and by dint of wearing her hat well on one side, to shut out all sight of the precipices, she gained the summit alive, though in need of refreshment, which Leonora administered in the form of raisins—offers of eau-de-Cologne and brandy being indignantly refused.

We sat down on the thick coarse turf, quite different from that on the other side, to enjoy the view, first noting that we had been one hour and ten minutes doing the last bit, and three and a half hours the whole ascent. The prospect before us was grand, though misty, and rapidly becoming more so. Foel Goch lay to the right, Y-Garn to the left, and straight in front our late toil was rewarded by the first sight of Snowdon, Elidyr, and countless heights and ridges; below were the grey waters of Llyn Peris, and Llanberis was just visible round the quarried terraces of Elidyr Fawr.

We took our bearings, and decided to make for Cwm Dudodyn, a long valley between Elidyr Fawr and an outlying ridge of Foel Goch, ending just above Llyn Peris. So down we went, over long slopes of grass, by no means interesting, and quite as tiring as the previous climbing, Leonora and Christina distinguishing themselves by attempting a short cut through a marsh. Ultimately we struck a convenient sheep-track, which in time became quite a respectable path, leading to a wall and gate near a clear little rill, where we halted to eat chocolate, and make use of the soap and towel, which Margery always carried in an underpocket.

We followed the path, fast narrowing into a mere track again, over and *through* a long stretch of boggy ground, which really was not worth the trouble of avoiding, as we had been wet so often in the course of the day, and presently saw on the opposite side of Dudodyn water a solitary angler, the first human be'ng we had encountered since leaving Ogwen.

D

After passing a sheepfold, the track became broad and plain, though rough, and led us at last into a hayfield, where a party of haymakers—men, girls, and children—were taking their afternoon meal. Finding that they had a little English, we entered into conversation, and bargained for some milk, which a picturesque child fetched from a cottage near by. To the delight of Christina and Constance, she brought butter-milk; but that beverage, though undoubtedly refreshing, did not commend itself to Margery and Leonora, so the girl was sent back for some fresh milk, which proved delicious.

After a little more talk with the haymakers, who were duly astonished on learning that we had come over the mountain from Ogwen, we continued our journey, still downhill, and soon gained the high-road, and Nant-Peris post-office, where we stopped to ask for letters and despatch some post-cards.

A little further on the road to Llanberis, we chanced on a pretty little house with a ticket in the window, announcing that tea was to be obtained within; so we availed ourselves of the invitation, and, for the modest sum of 8*d.* each, had quite a feast—tea, bread and butter, jam, and marmalade.

Tea over, we trudged along the high-road, feeling weary with Touchstone, if not with Rosalind, and stopping sometimes to look back at the Pass of

Llanberis, grand and gloomy in the gathering clouds, and again to notice the fine smoothed rocks, proving the former presence of glaciers.

Constance and Leonora were talking hard, and, as always happened when they got deep in conversation, unconsciously quickened their pace, leaving Margery and Christina behind taking a scientific interest in the rocks. A good half-mile from Nant-Peris Margery discovered that her shawl—a very precious one—was missing, and went back to the tea-house to look for it, leaving Christina to overtake the others. This she utterly failed to do, and was obliged to hire a small boy, whose legs she hoped were better than his English, to run after them. This he succeeded in doing, and a halt was made till Margery returned in triumph with the shawl; but, the extra mile having somehow given a final shake to her coiffure, a hasty toilette by the roadside was needed, as she had no mind to enter Llanberis school-girl fashion, with a pigtail down her back.

On the outskirts of Llanberis we spied a nice-looking cottage, or rather two cottages, which offered accommodation to travellers, and here we decided to pass the night. Before settling down, we walked through the little slaty town (slates *everywhere*, roofs, walls, steps, and the very paths of chipped slate), and then returned to find the inevitable ham and eggs waiting, to which we did full justice, and were soon ready for bed, Margery and Constance sleeping in a room behind the parlour, and Leonora and Christina going into the next cottage, where they found excellent accommodation.

CHAPTER VII.

LLANBERIS.

Friday, August 10.—We found ourselves more tired after the walk from Ogwen than we had expected, though we were neither footsore nor disagreeably sunburnt, so we agreed not to attempt Snowdon that day. We were influenced in making our decision by the prevailing mists, and later in the day were amply justified by drizzling rain.

Margery, being an early riser, acted as postman, but on arriving at the post-office at 8 a.m., when the delivery was supposed to begin, the letters were not sorted, and the obdurate official would not allow her to take away our parcels strewing the floor of the office; so she beguiled the time by explorations in the little town, and finally, near nine o'clock, set out for lodgings and breakfast. Wondering at her delay, Constance had started in the direction of the town, and presently they met, Margery being rejoiced to have help, as she was quite laden with parcels, containing more supplies of tea, chocolate, and other necessaries from home.

The morning was spent in writing and sewing, and various desultory expeditions in search of newspapers, provisions, and photographs. Leonora tried in vain to find a cobbler, but was told that all the men were haymaking, so she did a little necessary mending on her own account, and amused us all by using *white* thread, which she subsequently inked over.

The weather was too threatening to make a long expedition prudent, so in the afternoon we contented ourselves with a visit to a little glen just out of the town, whither we were guided by a friendly though somewhat officious little girl, whose absence we purchased by a stick of chocolate, as her appearance did not quite warrant the customary copper.

At the head of the glen we found a fine waterfall. The main body of the stream slides over a steep slope, and throws itself as a white mass into a deep, clear pool, the first of several similar pools of green water, with ferns and flowers growing on the banks as usual.

On leaving the glen, a desire for tea, and a pleasant recollection of yesterday's meal, led us to turn our steps towards Nant-Peris, whence we walked up the Pass of Llanberis, turning aside to see old Llanberis Church, which is nearly two miles distant from the new village and the well-known Snowdon ascent.

We found the church like others we had seen, very low-pitched, and not a little depressing in its general effect, though possessing various points of architectural interest, notably a curious fifteenth-century roof. Another singular feature was the presence of a large number of coffin-plates hanging on the western wall, and which had a very eerie appearance in the gathering dusk.

We did not linger long, as we found it impossible to gain any information from our guide, a little Welsh girl who had no English, though she was very friendly, and evidently appreciated Christina's " Diulch " (thank you) at the churchyard gate. In the churchyard we were pleased to note the neat appearance of the graves, which were in several cases planted with box, closely clipped into the form of a horizontal cross.

Soon after quitting the church, we attracted the attention of four small boys, who marched behind, whistling the " March of the Men of Harlech," until Leonora suddenly faced round and brandished her umbrella, when they precipitately fled.

Having performed this good office, Leonora turned back towards Llanberis; but the rest of us were tempted by the gloomy grandeur of the pass to extend our walk a little further, noting, as we strolled along, a resemblance in outline between the head of the valley and the Lake of Geneva. Margery thought the northern slopes of Snowdon above Llyn Peris not unlike the Savoy Alps, and the contour of the Glyders curiously like the Vaudois Alps, omitting the Dent du Midi.

The reflections in Llyn Peris were perfect; green slopes, white cottages, children at play, slopes of grey slate *débris*, were reduplicated below us.

The rapidly increasing gloom of the pass warned us that it was time to turn our steps towards Llanberis.

Even in the darkness our scientific instincts were on the alert, and Constance, noticing a curiously shaped tree-stump on the other side of the low wall marking off the road, advanced to examine it. To her surprise and dismay the supposed branches moved, and, reflecting that

> "He who fights and runs away,
> May live to fight another day,"

she retreated to safe quarters on the other side of the road. Margery and Christina, more valiant, went boldly up to the object, which, on close inspection, resolved itself into a horned black cow!

Certainly the creature looked more like one of the demon heads in Dürer's "Knight of Death" than was pleasant for feminine nerves in the dim light. By day we much admired the cattle, both black and red. We passed a specially fine herd between Capel Curig and Ogwen—all black—led by a bull with a splendid curly poll; but our admiration is distant, by preference, as we are never quite sure that their intentions are friendly.

A little reading, writing, and eating ended the somewhat uneventful day, which had, however, been very pleasant, and had enabled us entirely to recover from our recent exertions and fatigues.

CHAPTER VIII.

LLANBERIS TO BEDDGELERT VIÂ PEN-Y-GWRYD.

August 11, *Saturday.*—Another grey, rainy morning ruined our hopes of climbing Snowdon, so we decided to leave Llanberis and walk *viâ* Pen-y-gwryd to Beddgelert, and wait there for fairer skies. As the weather was so unfavourable, and the problem of wearing a knapsack *and* a waterproof difficult to solve, we arranged to send our packs by coach. Christina was unwilling to relinquish her "burden of many years," but we succeeded in convincing her that the knapsack was not the *raison d'être* of the tour, and her pack joined the others at the Royal Victoria Hotel, from which the Beddgelert coaches start.

We set out in the rain along the now familiar road to Nant-Peris, but the weather soon improved, though the sky remained grey enough to enhance the gloomy grandeur of the Pass of Llanberis. The Ogwen valley was scantily clothed with verdure, but here desolation reigned supreme. The rain and snow, frost and ice, have carved and peeled the lofty precipices and strewn the steep slopes with boulders of many curious shapes. Scarcely a flower or fern was to be seen, only in the little runnels by the wayside pale-green butterworts appeared to flourish, but their time of flowering was long past.

The road ascends steadily as far as Gorphwysfa, or Pen-y-pas, where one of the routes up Snowdon begins, and here we stayed to rest and exchange a few words with a party of ladies, including an Anglican Sister, who had driven through the pass just in advance of us, and who were kind enough to express admiration of our pedestrian powers.

After passing Gorphwysfa the road descends, and we were soon in sight of the Pen-y-gwryd Inn, where the road forks to Capel Curig and Beddgelert, and which has been made famous by its association with the honoured name of Charles Kingsley, who stayed there with Tom Hughes and Tom Taylor some thirty years ago.

The three recorded their holiday experiences in verse in the visitors' book, and if the holiday was as amusing as the verses, the friends must have had a very pleasant outing indeed. The original poem has fallen a victim to the predatory instincts of some visitor with hazy ideas of the difference between "mine" and "thine;" but fortunately a copy had been made, and the lines are probably familiar to all lovers of North Wales.

In case they are unknown to any of our readers, we will quote the first three verses as a sample of the excellence of the whole :—

T. T.

" I came to Pen-y-gwryd with colours armed and pencils,
But found no use whatever for any such utensils ;
So in default of them I took to using knives and forks,
And made successful drawings—of Mrs. Owen's corks.

C. K.

" I came to Pen-y-gwryd in frantic hopes of slaying
Grilse, Salmon, 3-lb. red-fleshed Trout, and what else there's no saying ;
But bitter cold and lashing rain, and black nor'-eastern skies, sir,
Drove me from Fish to botany, a sadder man and wiser.

T. H.

" I came to Pen-y-gwryd a-larking with my betters,
A mad wag and a mad poet, both of them men of letters ;
Which two ungrateful parties, after all the care I've took
Of them, make me write verses in Harry Owen's book."

But Kingsley's stay at Pen-y-gwryd is immortalized in literary material more lasting than nonsense verses, for every reader of " Two Years Ago " who has visited the neighbourhood of the Glyders will be able to realize the scenes therein described.

We entered the inn, which is still kept by Kingsley's host, Harry Owen, and ordered a more luxurious lunch than usual, in honour of the historic place in which we were to eat it.

While the meal was preparing we waited in the coffee-room, and, soon exhausting all the entertainment to be derived from the pictures and maps on the walls and the visitors' book, we turned our attention to the occupants of the chairs and sofas, and were speedily accosted by a clergyman, who was installed in a large armchair, trying to amuse himself with an old *Punch*. An exchange of civilities preluded an animated conversation, for our new acquaintance not only proved friendly and much disposed to talk, but, an experienced traveller, both able and willing to give us valuable information. He showed us some beautiful contour maps made by himself, and a book of clever sketches, which he brought under our notice with the careless remark, "Merely accurate, merely accurate;" but *we* thought the neat little pictures worthy of much praise, and wished we had such charming memorials of summer holidays, past and present.

We found out, thanks to Leonora's thorough and comprehensive study of one of the contour maps, that the owner of the map was familiar to us by repute as vicar of a South London parish, and more familiar still as brother of a lady famous in the educational world.

This discovery lent new zest to the conversation, and for some minutes we were decidedly "shoppy," despite muttered protests from Leonora. The arrival of our luncheon interrupted, but did not check the flow of talk, and before we had finished our coffee we had described in detail our climb from Ogwen to Llanberis, which was duly admired as an "eccentric little walk."

Our knapsacks were, of course, not *en évidence*, having gone on to Beddgelert, and as we discussed our past and future arrangements with an utter disregard of the question of luggage, some of our remarks must have been a little puzzling; but we did not think of this till afterwards. As a matter of fact, we had grown so used to consider our packs part of ourselves, that we should have been quite astonished if any one had suggested that we were not carrying them! In return for our confidences, Mr. —— told us that he had set himself the task of scaling the eleven mountains of 3000 feet in these parts, and had already done seven of them. We hoped he "worried through"—as he intended—to the end.

About 2.30 we left Pen-y-gwryd, and started off for Beddgelert, through a beautiful valley, the peaks and ridges of Snowdon forming one side, with innumerable streams dashing down to the Glaslyn, which, rising on Snowdon, comes tumbling down from Llyn Llydaw in a splendid series of falls, and runs through the valley to Llyn Gwynant and Llyn Dinas.

Later we had an opportunity of seeing the valley under happier circumstances, for on this occasion our line of vision was almost limited by our umbrellas, as the rain fell almost incessantly till we reached Beddgelert.

We kept up our spirits—and our skirts—as well as we could, and consoled ourselves with an occasional strawberry, and some chocolate, which we ate under a tree—only, somehow, even chocolate is not so very nice when the rain-drops are trickling down your neck, and finding a too convenient channel through the lace-holes of your boots.

Despite the downpour, Margery and Christina kept up their interest in science, gathered fine ferns and bunches of asphodel, and insisted on pointing out that the vegetation was changing with the altitude—that moorland flowers were being replaced by those common in meadows and hedgerows.

Leonora and Constance shared an umbrella, and the fragments of talk which were heard beyond its shelter were at one time far from cheerful. The words "loathed melancholy" reached Christina's ears, and Margery fancies that Constance's voice responded with various platitudes and quotations calculated to comfort, "Home-keeping youth have ever homely wits," and the like. Eventually the two under the umbrella got on to the truly feminine subject of clothes, and were smilingly indifferent to rain and its attendant evils.

We were all pleased when, after a couple of hours' walking, near the close of which the rain ceased, we came in sight of Beddgelert.

The little village stands right among the mountains, at the junction of the rivers Colwyn and Glaslyn. Craigwen, the very extremity of Snowdon, Moel Hebog, and Craig-y-llan dominate the three valleys, up and down which the roads to Carnarvon, Pen-y-gwryd, and Port Madoc respectively lead.

As usual, we went straight to the post-office, and there interviewed a polite but somewhat incoherent gentleman (who combines the office of postmaster with the direction of a grocery and drapery establishment) on the subject of letters, and any message from a landlady to whom we had written in advance.

The letters we got, but the message was a difficulty, which was solved on the arrival of more grocers and postmasters, members of the same family, equally polite, but still more incoherent and excited. After a babel of tongues, which defies description, we were on our way to our lodgings, and very satisfactory we found them.

After fetching our packs from the Goat, where

they had been dropped by the coach, we had tea, and then settled down to enjoy the delightful view from our parlour window.

We overlooked the rushing Colwyn, and its stone bridge—evidently the regular village lounging-place—and had beyond a glimpse of the church, then Moel Hebog and Craig-y-llan, and between these the entrance to the far-famed Aberglaslyn valley.

Leonora left us to search for a cobbler to mend her boot, the amateur workmanship not having proved a complete success.

During her absence we inspected our hats, with the view of ascertaining the amount of damage they had sustained in the rain. They certainly did not present a very correct Sunday-go-to-meeting appearance, and we found it necessary to take off the scarves, borrow an iron, and busy ourselves with millinery till supper-time.

Leonora returned in triumph, having, after some search, found a most satisfactory shoemaker—Welsh, it is true, and unable to speak English, but signs had sufficed to explain what the boot needed, and constant reiteration had, she thought, fully impressed him with the fact that the boot must be done *at once*, as she had no second pair. Later we despatched a maid with the boot, and hoped for the best, but we had to live in hope till the following morning.

CHAPTER IX.

BEDDGELERT.

Sunday, August 12.—A stormy night was succeeded by a thoroughly wet morning, and by breakfast-time the village street was in a fair way to become a watercourse.

Another unpleasant fact greeted Leonora when she put in a tardy appearance at breakfast. Either the cobbler had proved faithless, or, as was more probable, she had over-rated her power of giving instructions in an unknown tongue, for the boot was not forthcoming. After a few minutes of anxious suspense, during which we were oppressed by the fear that poor Leonora would be a prisoner all day, we learned that the boot was still in the house, the cobbler having declined to undertake the job till Monday, when he really grasped what was required of him.

When the hour of morning service approached, the rain was still falling, but we braved the elements; Margery and Constance started for the parish church,

Leonora and Christina directed their steps towards one of the numerous chapels we had noticed the day before.

On joining forces again, the church-goers reported favourably of the service they had attended, though the congregation was small, and the accent of vicar and choir struck English ears somewhat unpleasantly.

The chapel was a pleasant little building, quite small, yet a world too wide for the congregation, who numbered seventeen. However, if the quantity was small, the quality was good, for out of these seventeen persons eight were grown men. The scanty attendance was possibly explained by an announcement from the pulpit that this was the first service in English this season, and was intended for the convenience of visitors, who would, it was hoped, contribute, etc. When a hymn was given out, Leonora and Christina realized that they occupied the distinguished position of sole representatives of the English nation, for the harmonium was almost entirely unsupported by the congregation; and the two deacons, who stood on either side of the minister, did not even go through the farce of opening their hymn-books, and it was clearly evident that a very small proportion indeed of the seventeen had any acquaintance with English.

The sermon was excellent, carefully prepared, with allusions to England, and carefully read, but difficult to follow, as *t*'s and *d*'s, *c*'s and *g*'s, *p*'s and *b*'s were hopelessly confused.

After church, as the weather was better, we had a short stroll up the Carnarvon road, and after dinner a longer one in the same direction. The country is bleak and wild, and appeared additionally so in the stormy weather, the wind blowing so hard that we saw some haycocks actually carried away.

Another Y-Garn, and a fine group of heights with Hebog lie on the right of the road, and Craigwen, Y Aran, and Llechog—all peaks or spurs of Snowdon—bound it on the right. About two and a half miles distant from Beddgelert is a curious profile rock, easy to recognize as Pitt's Head, and indeed impossible to pass unnoticed, for the words "Pitt's Head" are painted in great white letters on the side of the rock, and painfully remind the rest-seeking tourist of "Willing" and "Colman's Mustard."

Another rock near at hand has been treated in the same manner, but in that case the hieroglyphics are incomprehensible to the Sassenach. We were told that the odd white letters marked the spot where a famous horse made a famous leap, but to critical eyes the leap appears so incredible that we ceased to be surprised that the fact was noted in an unknown tongue.

CHAPTER X.

BEDDGELERT (*Continued*).

Monday, August 13.—The gale which sprang up last evening had moderated but slightly during the night. After breakfast, however, the sun came out, so, when certain needful mending had been done, we started off down the Aberglaslyn Pass, hoping to have a sight of Gelert's grave, but the oft-described spot is now so very inconspicuous that we never descried it, and, after sundry fruitless attempts to localize the faithful hound's last resting-place, we turned our attention to the pass which lay before us, and which, though short, is certainly very fine. The Glaslyn river makes the most of its rocky bed; and the rocky walls, though very close to the road, allow of some fine groups and stretches of firs and other trees. Just at the right place (from an artist's point of view) there is a bridge, Pont Aberglaslyn, where the road to Maentwrog and Festiniog branches off, leaving the main road to go on to Port Madoc and the sea. The best view of the pass is from the bridge, with the foaming stream in the foreground. The bridge itself, massive and hoary with lichens, ferns, and creepers, adds no little to the effect when viewed from the road or the rocky bank below.

After dinner we started for Moel Hebog, having first consulted our landlady as to the best route, and bearing in mind a remark of our clerical acquaintance at Pen-y-gwryd, that "Moel Hebog was only a turfy mountain, and we should easily walk over *that;*" but experience disproved the truth of the remark, for *us* at least, for turf is apt to be boggy, and often much harder climbing than boulders—at least, so we found, and, with the wind still high, Hebog proved more than a match for us, as the sequel will show.

First we traversed a little wood, from which, when we had climbed a very little way, we had a grand view of Snowdon's mass, all but Y-Wyddfa, the central peak, which was still in the clouds. Then we mounted over pastures and rock, more and more mountains coming into view at every step. There was no semblance of track, after the little wood, so we made our way as best we could up to a prominent spur of the mountain, where our progress was stopped by an unusually high and solid wall, with pointed stones forming a kind of *chevaux de frise* along its top. But the top formed such an excellent vantage-ground, that Margery, finding a possible place to scale the wall, mounted it to reconnoitre, while the others rested from their labours. The strong wind made our progress slow and toilsome, but, the wall once surmounted, we plodded on, after making a circuit to avoid a thorough wetting in the bogs—*damp* we were, as usual. By degrees we worked our way round to the north-east shoulder of the mountain, about three-quarters of the way up, where we finally halted, as the wind was too high to make it safe for us to try the rest of the ascent. Thence, however, the view was magnificent, quite the most extensive we had seen.

The mountain mass is detached (like the Rigi), so one gets views in all directions. To our right (the south-west), as we sat, was the sea-shore—miles of it, Tremadoc and Cardigan Bays—perhaps St. David's Head, but we were not quite sure of that; Harlech lying below us. Inland was the Aberglaslyn Pass and the ridges towards Festiniog, with many further heights not named in our map. Nearer, looking south-eastwards, the jagged mass of Moelwyn, overlooking Festiniog; in the foreground (beyond Hebog's slopes and the deep gorge of the Glaslyn), the heathery ridge of Craig-y-llan, which forms the eastern side of the Aberglaslyn Pass; over this, and much further off, Moel Siabod (pronounced *Shabbod*), which we had partly seen at Capel Curig, raising a splendid curved crest, and sloping down to the Nant-Gwynant and its lakes, by which we had passed on Saturday from Pen-y-gwryd. Both lakes were visible, and the road past them, and Beddgelert's roofs right below us. Bits of the Carnedd range filled up the corner between Siabod and Snowdon's mass, now at last revealed in all its grandeur; Y-Wyddfa, with its tremendous hollow; Aran's peak; the splendid serrated crest of Lliwedd; and between this and Y-Wyddfa, quite clearly visible, the triple peak of our old friend Y-Garn, over Ogwen. Craigwen's pastures and the Colwyn valley lay wide to our left, the Carnarvon road stretching on to Llyn-y-Gader, and the view was bounded by the rest of Snowdon's mass, over a ridge of which we saw, a little later, when we had changed our position to the north-westward, Elidyr Fawr and the slate quarries over Llyn Peris.

The descent from Hebog was long and rather wearisome, over boggy pastures and slopes, but we had fine views all the way, and finally arrived in the Carnarvon road, after successfully dodging a ferocious-looking dog, which seemed to have very clear ideas on the law of trespass. The sunset over Hebog and the western Y-Garn was grand—the sky piled up with huge, smoky, red clouds; then the wind dropped, and a calm evening was the precursor of the most glorious day of our whole expedition.

CHAPTER XI.

BEDDGELERT TO PENRHYN-DEUDRAETH AND SNOWDON.

Tuesday, August 14.—We were called at 5.20 a.m., packed, breakfasted, and drove off to Pitt's Head (two and a half miles up the Carnarvon road), to begin the long-hoped-for ascent of Snowdon.

Having thus saved ourselves a bit of road we had already seen twice, we left it at 7.15 a.m., and made for Llechog, Snowdon's shoulder, which lay before us. The track is first a farm road; then leads over *very* boggy meadows; then rough, stony pastures, where it requires the closest inspection, and often a vivid imagination. Margery, being the most used to mountaineering, usually led, and brought us out into the Pont Rhyddu track, which is now considered one of the best ways of approaching the summit. It is plain enough; a good, though at times a rough path, being made of splinters of stone nearly all the way. It winds in zigzags slowly up the huge shoulder, with very little view in front, the summit invisible, but on all other sides grand views opening out at every step —the road we had left, with Hebog, Y-Garn, and lakes Gader and Cwellyn below; then the Nantlle valley and its lakes; between Moel Eilio and Mynydd Maur, Carnarvon Castle quite distinct for a while, with Anglesey and Holyhead beyond. Then Beaumaris Bay came in sight, and the Menai bridge; then Tremadoc Bay (over Hebog's shoulders), and the coast far away to Aberystwith, etc. Up and up we went, the wind being north-west and fresh; we were cool most of the way, and it was still early when we neared the summit, having first to cross a long narrow ridge, the Bwlch-y-maen, where the path, though narrow, is firm and good, and the views down each side, of the cwms and llyns below, splendid. Siabod now rose grandly, and many further heights, while we were close to the huge ridge of Lliwedd, which runs down into Nant-Gwynant. Up still, and into the clouds which persistently hung over the summit, till we reached the Cairn and huts, to find ourselves actually the only visitors, and this on a fine day, in the height of the season! We ascertained that *one* gentleman had spent the night on the top in order to see (?) the sun rise; but he had departed, and so we had the summit practically to ourselves. There was no view from the very top, however, so we recorded our names, eat a little of the food we had brought, wrapped ourselves up (for the mist was very chilly), and about ten o'clock proceeded down the other side, without waiting for the mist to clear, as we were anxious to catch the coach at Pen-y-gwryd. We were very soon below the cloud, and the views were splendid again over Llanberis and Llyn Padarn, Elidyr Fawr, and the ridges and crests of Dydisgyl and Crib Goch, with Llyn Glaslyn below in the huge hollow of Y-Wyddfa.

We followed the Llanberis path (a good broad *road* it is!) rather further than we needed, to see again the Cwm Dudodyn and the ridge of Foel Goch—the scene of our exploits on the way to Llanberis.

Then we descended by long zigzags over a rough and narrow but safe path, right down the slope that joins Y-Wyddfa and Crib Goch, to near the lakes Glaslyn and Llydaw, so deep and changeful in colour—now grey, now dimpling, now blue as the sky above, though that was often covered by passing clouds, for which we were not sorry. The mountain-side is bare of interesting plants, near the path, at any rate; but we picked up pretty pieces of quartz and other minerals from among the *débris* that were gradually sliding (apparently) down to the water below. We ought to have seen, on the opposite side of the cwm, the cross recently erected on the spot where Mr. Evans lost his life earlier in the season; we read the account of the sad mishap in the "locked book," sacred to descriptions of mountaineering exploits and scientific notes, which is kept at Pen-y-gwryd Inn, but we failed to sight the monument among the rocks on the mountain-side.

We could not take the usual broad track to Gorphwysfa, for the causeway which crosses Llydaw was deep under water this season, as we had heard, happily, from our kind clerical friend at Pen-y-gwryd, for a boy whom we questioned at the top could give us no information worth having. We took the upper path, therefore; it is narrow, and often very wet—as indeed we found all the paths that day—but quite distinct and easy, so that we were much amused at meeting a party of tourists—*men* only—with a guide! Just where we passed them, the path led over a broad, smooth slab of rock, where one of the tourists, a middle-aged man, stopped dead, and declared that he couldn't see the path and daren't go any further! till reassured by the guide, who greeted us respectfully, and asked for the latest news from the summit, our appearance (though we were minus our packs) evidently causing much interest to the party. A little further we saw a large party of people, with ladies and children, evidently *un*guided, for they were on the lower road, and, being stopped by the lake, were making a toilsome *détour* round its shore to rejoin the path. We were too far to shout directions, so we had to leave them to their fate—probably a bog, towards which they were obviously wending their way. Moral—don't go up Snowdon in a rainy season without hints from a mountaineering friend.

We succeeded, with care, in keeping fairly dry; reached Gorphwysfa at 12.45 p.m., trotted down to Pen-y-gwryd, having had lovely views of Lakes Padarn and Peris—blue as the sky that day—and found that the last coach for Beddgelert had left five minutes before! However, Harry Owen, junior, was equal to the occasion; a waggonette (which cost the same as the coach-fare for the party) soon appeared at the door, while we had lunch, wrote in the visitors' book —a ceremony we quite forgot on our former visit— inquired after our kind clerical friend, who had not yet returned from "worrying through" the rest of the summits over 3000 feet, and started again at 2.15 for a delicious drive down to Beddgelert—mountains clear all the way, for Snowdon uncovered his crown finally an hour after we left the top.

Arrived at Plas Gwyn, we arranged and shouldered our packs, bid kind Mrs. Thomas good-bye, received her hearty good wishes for the remainder of our journey, and departed down the Aberglaslyn pass, the whole valley glowing in the afternoon sunshine.

We were bound for Tan-y-bwlch, on the way to Festiniog, so we crossed the river, and took the road to the left—a delightful walk of seven and a half miles, during which we camped once to make tea and enjoy it. The road, solitary as usual, took us over the border of Merionethshire, and into quite a different kind of country from that we had previously traversed, much of it being land reclaimed from bogs, or the sea, or ancient lake-bottoms, now forming level pastures, of the richest green, while here and there haymakers were still busy, making pretty groups in the glowing light—such a golden green as one rarely sees over the border. The sides of the valley, evidently once a llyn or fiord, are hills, either wooded (chiefly with oaks) or bare, often showing very strikingly the smoothing of ancient ice. Over the lower hills rise the peaks of the Moelwyns, especially Cynicht, whose ridge ends in a pyramidal peak, *very* like a small Matterhorn, and, seen in the evening light, with deep purple shadows clearly defining its ridges, a most striking object. Looking back over the "traeth," or reclaimed land, especially near the end of the day, the whole mass of Snowdon made a grand purple "silhouette" against the clear evening sky—no details visible, but just a magnificent outline, the serrated edge of the Bwlch-y-maen we had traversed in the morning being especially conspicuous. This crowning group was worthily supported by Hebog's mass to the left, and the Moelwyns and Cynicht to the right; we had constantly to turn and look at it, and at the sheets of green in the foreground, the groups of fir, beech, oak, birch in the middle distance, and ferns and wild flowers everywhere. A few farms and two roadside inns, with the usual white-walled, grey-roofed, one-storied cottages, were all the houses we passed for miles, and we hardly met a soul along the road.

At Llanfrothen post-office, situated in what we, from our map, took to be the village of that ilk, the road forked, and we, still following our map, struck right across the traeth, by a straight dyked road. Far to the right, with our backs to Snowdon, we saw the chimneys and smoke of Port Madoc, close to the sea. The roads puzzled us a little, but the one we followed was evidently a main road, and seemed to fit one on our map so well that we pursued it two miles or more farther, and then, after mounting a wooded hill, and enjoying one last glorious sight of Snowdon, we descended to a village, whence we saw the sea, or an estuary, quite close, and Harlech towers plainly visible. This was *too* much, for we ought still to have been among the mountains! Seeing a gentleman in clerical costume just ahead of us, Margery went up to him and inquired our whereabouts, and he soon explained (in English which, though very *Welsh*, was intelligible) that we had come wrong ever since Llanfrothen, or rather Gareg, as the hamlet is called.

The mistake was entirely owing to our road (made sixty years ago) being omitted from the ordnance map, "corrected" down to 1883! Well, we were now several miles from Tan-y-bwlch, our intended destination; the sun was almost down, and we were fairly tired; so, after achieving the name, Penrhyn-deudraeth, of the village in which we had landed, we asked our clerical friend if he could recommend us a lodging. He at once stepped up to a woman, wearing the "fore-and-aft" cap (which is nearly as much affected by the natives as by the visitors), and leaning over her gate close by. After a brief but animated Welsh conversation, Mr. X. (we learned his name later) announced to us "Miss Jones" would be happy to give us quarters, provided we could make two rooms do. To this we at once agreed, and were assured that the house was very clean, and the beds "airy"! We found ourselves heartily welcomed, and very comfortable.

The sun was just setting; a low rocky ridge lies on the farther side of the estuary, above which stands the house, and soon a perfect "alpen-glühen" spread its rosy glow over the grey rocks.

Going indoors, after enjoying this peep at Alpine scenery, as it were, we contrived, with care, for Miss Jones's stock of English is limited, to make her understand our wants in the way of supper, and soon ham and eggs were frizzling cheerily in the comfortable, exquisitely neat "house-place." As it is a type of many others we glanced at on the way, doors generally being wide open, this one is worth describing. It is entered straight, by slate steps and a porch, from the little garden; the wide fireplace is guarded by an iron "fire-stool," and near it is placed a broad, high-backed settle with cushion; against the wall is a tall dresser, well garnished with blue plates and dishes and shining glasses, for which the dark wood forms an admirable background. The floor is of broad slates; a few chairs, a table or two, and a tall clock (suggestive of one of the best of the Ingoldsby Legends, whose scene is laid in the Principality), complete the furniture. Exactly opposite the door, a tiny staircase leads to the upper rooms. Miss Jones had a little parlour also, and a shop, for she dealt in flour and bread, and the latter was delicious, as we proved ere long. Our rooms were very tiny, but nice, and by keeping the windows open we had air enough.

While the others were unpacking, Margery interviewed Miss Jones, and most of the house, including the flour-sacks. Presently Mr. X. reappeared, so she fetched our ordnance map-sheets, and, taking advantage of a broad, low slate wall in front of the house, spread out the sheets, and Mr. X. kindly corrected them in pencil. Now, it had dawned upon

Leonora that our unknown benefactor bore a striking resemblance to one of the preachers we had heard the Sunday before at Beddgelert, so Margery gently worked the conversation round, till the identity was proved. He had also recognized Leonora and Christina, and, having heard that the former had taken shorthand notes of his discourse, would fain have made further acquaintance with his fair reporter. But *that* pleasure was denied him.

Beside Mr. X., who seemed quite at home in Miss Jones's house-place, there appeared also a young schoolmaster, belonging in some way to Beddgelert, but lodging in the house. He very kindly agreed to convey back to Mrs. Thomas a knife we had carried off by mistake. After making this and sundry other arrangements for the morning, we retired to our "airy" beds, to enjoy what we deemed well-earned repose. It certainly seemed more than a day since we first left Beddgelert in the early morning! But greater toils were in store for us on the morrow!

CHAPTER XII.

PENRHYN TO DOLGELLY VIÂ FESTINIOG AND THE MOUNT MORGAN GOLD MINE.

Wednesday, August 15.—The next morning was cloudy, but fine.

We regained consciousness about seven, Constance and Leonora requiring a certain amount of friendly help from the rest of the party, and, after bidding a very hearty good-bye to Miss Jones, we embarked on the curious little " toy railway," which passes in front of the house. The gauge of this railway is only two feet, it having been planned originally only to carry slates. The engines are remarkably powerful, but everything is on a small scale except the passenger-carriages, which, though low, are broad and comfortable. But the cuttings are only just wide enough to admit the train, and not an inch more than is needed has been cut away for the tunnels. Somebody told the story of the Frenchman who, showing an inclination to admire the view in similar circumstances, was cautioned to "look out," which he hastily did, and so came to a tragic end. The curves of the line are very sharp, the gradients very steep, and the trains very long. Going round some curves, we could easily see the engine a-head of us, and the guard's van behind, and thus were able, to some slight degree, to understand the universal desire of kittens to catch their respective tails. We passed one long train of full slate trucks, running down from Blaenau-Festiniog, where the chief quarries are, without any engine, and with a man at the brake here and there along the trucks. The line runs up and down the mountains, and round or across the "traeths," in a charming way, and we were very glad to have been on it. At Blaenau-Festiniog we changed for Festiniog village, *viâ* Great Western Railway, which also curves finely on its way south.

At Festiniog we shouldered our knapsacks and set out for Dolgelly. The day was still cloudy and not very attractive; nor was the road itself very interesting, being a high road between walls, and evidently not one of Telford's. We also felt much aggrieved at finding no milestones, which always have a wonderfully inspiring effect on us. But in spite of the drawbacks, there were several objects of interest around us, and, looking south, we had pretty peeps towards the sea; north-west runs a long line of barren rounded hills, the Manods and Mynydds, with fine outlines, and our friend Hebog generally in view ; Siabod to the north-east, and Snowdon visible near the end of the day. Our botanists noted ferns, especially blechnum, lady ferns (cut for fodder), flowers of a semi-lowland character, including harebells (blue and white), willow-leaved spirea, asphodel, bog-myrtle, and yellow pansies. *In* the road, some two or three miles from Festiniog, are iron springs, which, when there is not too much slope or traffic, make great orange gelatinous patches, which bubble and crackle when stirred.

On we plodded, until we reached a village, Trawsfynydd, where we learnt that we were five, and not, as, we had fondly hoped, seven miles from Festiniog. Moreover, our day's walk, which had been calculated at thirteen miles, now promised to be eighteen at least. Christina, who was responsible for the calculation, was made to regret it. We laid in a store of provisions, stowed them away in the "washing-bag," and set out to cover the weary stretch of road before us. This "washing-bag" had been dubbed so by Constance, whose pet abhorrence it was. It was not very large, but was made of brown holland, that being the only material at hand on the evening before our start, when the suggestion was made that "a bag of some kind would be very useful."

Our way was rendered less monotonous by the

kindness of an intelligent policeman, who drew us a map of another and more interesting road over the mountains, which would take us beside two waterfalls and the Pritchard-Morgan gold mine. A little distance along this new road, which, however, is old and probably Roman, we passed a number of haymakers, who all turned out in a row to gaze. Before long we found a soft green slope and a little rill, where we lunched, rested, and watched some pretty geese make their toilet at the rill. A young miner came by, and told us which road to take, as they forked just below. Then we passed an old ruined chapel and graveyard; some of the tombstones looked new, but we hardly saw a house for miles. Some time before, we had passed another chapel used as a carpenter's shop, with a coffin being made in it. On and on, over bare hillsides, with a few sheep feeding about; then over a little river; then up again. Suddenly we came in sight of a well-wooded glen, and, stretching up its sides, some evidently new mining works, which we concluded must be the famous Pritchard-Morgan gold mines. We went down the path, entered the enclosure, and while Leonora, Christina, and Constance rested for a time, Margery, seeing some workmen at a short distance, offered to go and get some information from them. They could give but little, and, on Margery's asking if Mr. Morgan were there, or if we should be allowed to see any of the workings, referred her to the captain of the mine, who was standing in a group of three or four near some sheds down below us. There was nothing for it but to go to them, and accordingly she made her way down by a rough, steep path. Landing safely, however, at the bottom, she went up to the group, who were bending with eager interest over some newly washed mineral specimens. On her asking for the "captain," he looked up, a big fair-bearded man in a miner's jacket; but a gentleman close to Margery at once said, " I am the chairman; shall I do as well?" She explained how we came to be there, and asked if we might see any portion of the workings. Thereupon the captain remarked that there was a fee for going into the mine (we learned afterwards that a fee of ten shillings has been charged lately to parties of visitors, and devoted to the Miners' Benevolent Fund—of this we knew nothing at the time). Before Margery could reply, the chairman said he thought the specimens they had there were the most interesting part, at the same time showing her quartz with various other minerals, some pieces having gold encrusting the quartz. The gold is seen in little tree-like masses, or like very yellow crumb of bread, sticking to black or white rock, rather difficult to describe, but, once seen, easily recognized, at least in such quantities as we saw it. Margery had seen Australian specimens, and knew what to expect; but, aware that the others had not been so fortunate, she beckoned to the three to come down, and as they arrived some more gentlemen appeared, one of whom the chairman introduced as his brother, a Queensland gold-digger. While we were all standing round the specimens, the chairman said that the directors, who had held a meeting previous to our arrival, were going into the mine, and offered to let us accompany them. Naturally we were not loth to avail ourselves of such kindness, though we were anxious not to be in the way. We quite understood that visitors might be undesirable, and were the more delighted at such an unexpected opportunity having arisen.

We were warned that the mine was very wet and dirty, but that did not deter us from penetrating into its depths. The gentlemen retired into the office to transform themselves into miners, while we unstrapped our packs, tucked up our skirts, put on our cloaks, and dispensed with our hats. Margery tied a neckerchief over her head, Leonora put on a woollen cap, while Christina and Constance borrowed caps from the office. Then, having been provided with candles all round, we were ready.

We entered the mine by a horizontal gallery, out of which a tramway runs, conveying the ore to the mill further down the glen. The gentlemen went first, the chairman kindly taking charge of us. We soon reached a short vertical shaft, part of the older workings, which were stopped some five and twenty years ago. They showed us the "reef" of quartz rock, resting against or upon the dark "foot-wall," a layer of rock near which the richer ore is always found. Close to us a new shaft was being sunk, and into it the chairman, another gentleman, and the captain were swung in a bucket, to see the place where the captain had noticed some "colour," *i.e.* gold.

While we waited, some one remarked that it would be dangerous to let anything fall down the shaft; to which the gold-digger brother replied that he had known of a man being killed by a pound of candles falling on his head. He went on to say that he remembered a man (in Queensland, we suppose) on whose head a tin can or bucket was dropped from a great height. Happily the rim at the bottom did not hit him, or he would have been killed, but his head went right through the bottom of the can ! The poor fellow was indeed "in a box," for the iron rim was too hard for the onlookers to open, and they had to lead him three-quarters of a mile, with his head in the can, shouting with pain, and probably some other feeling, until he could be released from his unpleasant predicament.

In process of time, the captain was pumped up, and was soon followed by the others. We all relighted our candles, the miners carrying theirs in a lump of clay, which they stick on the rock when they want to use both hands. By their glimmering light we proceeded along the now pitch-dark gallery, splashing through the pools of water between the sleepers of the tramway, and avoiding the places where the ore is shot down from the upper galleries. These galleries are driven either along or across the quartz reefs; this one seemed to go along the reef.

And now came the "crux" of the matter as regards difficulty, for we were to ascend to the upper gallery, and the only means of doing so was what may be best described as a spiral staircase with the steps omitted—a short, steep incline of loose, shifting *débris*, with here and there a beam stretching right across, which had in most cases to be crawled under, then a turn, and at last, by dint of clambering, pulling, and pushing, we scrambled up to the higher working, where we came to the end of a gallery, with two or three miners at work in it. There we were shown the rich ore *in situ*, close against the foot-wall. Our space was very circumscribed. The directors, the mine-manager, the captain, our four selves, and the miners, all with candles, were crowded together into a space not more than ten feet square, and barely six feet high; and yet the air was neither hot nor unpleasant. The ventilation seemed good all through, and the water from the upper workings drains off through the lower—an advantage derived from the situation of the mine on a slope. Water dripped all round, and the footwall, which there forms one side of the gallery, being very black and crumbly, soon disguised the colour of our hands. That did not matter! We looked and listened, and kept ourselves as much out of the way as possible. Both the chairman and the manager were very kind in showing us everything of interest, and in answering our questions. We saw lead, arsenic, zinc, copper, and iron ores in the rock, and heard that silver is occasionally found with the lead, and that manganese also occurs sparingly. Blende is, in this mine, a sure sign of the presence of rich ore in the neighbourhood. Black slate, breaking into the reef as a vein (called by the miners a "horse") is also a good sign. We saw one in the roof of the working.

We had not been long in the gallery, when two blasts were fired above us; the sound, however, was not very loud. The explosive used is gelatine dynamite, in quantity sufficient to loosen half a ton of rock at a time. After blasting, the poorer ore is sent off in the tram-waggons, the richer pieces, or "pockets," being carefully removed and kept apart. The day before our visit, the chairman had taken out four hundred pounds' worth of gold, from a spot shown us, and another "pocket" was ready for the directors to inspect. The mere mention of it seemed to put them on their mettle, and they set to work, first with their hands, then the captain plied his crowbar, bringing down some of the rock already loosened by the blasts, and finally the ex-golddigger took a pick (remarking as he did so that a sharp one was rarely to be seen in a gold mine, on account of the hard quartz rock), and wielded it with great skill, the miners looking on in a grimly amused sort of way. The men are mostly Welsh, and paid by the day—three shillings and sixpence per day; they work on eight-hour shifts, night and day.

The manager is from California, and intends to work the mine thoroughly on the Californian plan. New machinery is to be at once introduced, to diminish the cost of working. As the directors were likely to stay a long while at the pocket, the manager, knowing that we had still a good walk before us, proposed our going on. So we bade them good-bye, with gritty hand-shakes, and many thanks for their kindness, which we appreciated the more when we learned that, half an hour before we appeared on the scene, the directors had made a rule forbidding the manager to admit visitors, the work being so much hindered by them. So we may be the last visitors to see the working for some time to come.

We were taken into another gallery on our way out, where blasting had just taken place, and this was the only part of the mine where the air was in the least unpleasant, being thick with fumes. We noticed afterwards that the water dripping from the rock had evidently exercised a solvent action on the rubber of our mackintoshes, as we found them full of little holes, and the binding at the bottom had become loose and was peeling off; while Margery's woollen cloak was, after brushing, none the worse for the expedition.

Emerging to the daylight, we were taken to the office to wash and reassume a respectable appearance. We had rather a small allowance of water, the fact being, as the manager observed, that every available vessel was in use for washing specimens. However, with our own towel and soap we got off the worst of the mud, and departed, armed with a note of introduction to the manager of the stamping-mill below. We were put in charge of a well-dressed young fellow who was strolling about, with no apparent occupation. We discovered, on the way down, that he was a constable, whose sole business it is to watch the men as they come from work, to see that they carry off no gold.

Reaching the stamping-mill and producing our order, the manager of that department took us over the mill, and partly showed, partly explained, the following processes:—

1. The rough ore, brought down by the tramway, is shot into a hopper, and broken into pieces about the size of a small apple.

2. The ore, thus broken, is passed under heavy metal stampers, working alternately, and ground by degrees into the finest mud.

3. This mud is slowly carried by a current of water over copper plates coated with mercury, which takes up the gold, allowing the refuse to pass on.

4. The amalgam of mercury and gold, when enough has been collected from the plates and batteries, is placed in retorts, the mercury driven off by heat, and the gold remaining fused into "bricks," or ingots.

This fourth part of the process we did not see, nor the finished ingots, as the key of that part of the building had been left up at the mine.

The inferior ore is passed over a machine, which by gentle shaking separates the heavier part (ores of lead, zinc, and iron pyrites, with any gold or silver they contain) from the lighter quartz, etc. This metallic mud is shipped off to be dealt with by a different process. The noise of the machinery was so great that much of the explanation had to be given by pantomime.

The mill is situated in a beautiful part of the glen, between two waterfalls, the Rhaiadr Mawddach and the Pistil-y-cain, whose respective streams join just below the mill. Advantage is taken of the falls to turn a great waterwheel, which sets going all the machinery of the mill. The pretty glen is being sadly spoiled by the mining operations, and the waters of the Mawddach are discoloured for miles below the mill. We had learned from the mine-manager that the mine had been deserted for over twenty years, being never properly and systematically worked; that after Mr. Pritchard Morgan had proved its worth, he had disposed of the property to a company the previous June, himself remaining a large shareholder. The present working is very successful, though of course the reef is not uniformly rich.

After the mill-manager had showed us the two waterfalls, he dismissed us down the tramway of a powder-mill not then at work.

Constance had picked up a very pretty bit of quartz with ore (probably iron pyrites) on Snowdon the day before. The tints of the ore are rather unusual, so, while in the mine, we showed it to the directors, who were amused to find we had been "prospecting on Snowdon," and intended to examine the interesting and "knowing-looking" specimen in daylight; but, as we were the first to leave the mine, we are still in ignorance as to the possible riches of the Welsh monarch.

It was 6.30 when we left the mill, having reached the mine some two hours before, and we had still eight or nine miles to go. First our way lay down the tramlines, and then along a very good road parallel to the torrent, and through the woods to the high-road we had left some hours earlier. It is prettier here, being overhung by trees. Here again the milestones are very defective, so we had to ask our way repeatedly. The cottagers speak little or no English; but by dint of names of places and much pantomime, we got our directions, and in one place a drink of buttermilk and some water. It grew darker and darker, and on we sped, doing our seventeenth mile in twelve minutes, with a downward slope to help us. We grew *very* hungry, and eat raisins, biscuits, and chocolate as we walked. On still, till the road forked. Happily we found a cottage at the turn, and a rap with an umbrella brought out two dear old women, capped and hatted—do they always wear their hats?—who, with beaming smiles, pointed out our right road, although they had "dim Sassenach" (no English). The road was very good, happily, for we were getting terribly tired, and stumbled over any little stone. Two miles from the friendly old women and twenty-one from Festiniog, we came down into Dolgelly, just as the church bell was ringing for nine o'clock—so we had done about nine miles in two hours and a half. As usual we made for the post-office, but it was closed. It was quite too late to look for rooms, but we found comfortable quarters in a "Temperance" near at hand. Oh, how glad we were of the chops and delicious coffee with which we were provided!

CHAPTER XIII.

DOLGELLY.

Thursday, August 16.—After a very late breakfast, Leonora went out to the post, but omitted to take her bearings, and so had to find her way back by the knowledge she had acquired the night before. This amounted to "Jones's Temperance." Leonora maintains that every other house in the street is a "Temperance," and that they are all kept by Joneses. We have verified this in three cases, which make the state of affairs quite confusing enough. These "Temperances" simply *swarm;* other "publics" are few. Chapels abound; the tiniest village has two at least, and one finds them in curious lonely places as well. In the case of Dolgelly, this is not surprising if the services of the parish church at all correspond with the building. It is hideous, and very depressing.

About noon we set out for the "Torrent Walk," a very pretty ravine, where the stream runs among mossy boulders, with trees and ferns everywhere.

Margery again found hymenophyllum (filmy fern) and lovely mosses. We selected a quiet spot in which to eat our lunch, and spent the afternoon in sketching, reading, writing, and resting.

We were sorry not to have had time to see more of Dolgelly and its surroundings. It is a curious little town ; the streets are very winding, and the grey stone houses are stuck down anyhow and anywhere. They have dormer windows by way of upper storey, which give them a quaint, old-world, sleepy look. There is only one post out and one in, but two banks, and at least two chemists. A curious contrast !

CHAPTER XIV.

DOLGELLY TO BARMOUTH VIÂ CADER IDRIS AND ARTHOG.

Friday, August 17.—The morning was grey and hazy, but the wind was fresh and east, so we had hopes of a good day. After laying in a stock of provisions, we went up the town, and along the Towyn road for three miles. On turning up Cader, we found the many possible paths rather confusing, and so gladly followed a party led by a guide. After a time this grew tiresome, so we took the lead, the path being more evident.

At first the way lies south, over pastures, but soon it becomes rough and stony, and it is bad nearly all the way up. A steep climb leads to a ridge connecting two of the chief peaks of the range, then east along a level stretch, and then another long disagreeable and uninteresting climb brings one up to the cairn, from which the view must certainly be fine in clear weather, but we were very unfortunate.

There are some deep cwms and two llyns, but they are small, and not nearly so striking as Idwal, Ogwen Glaslyn, or Llydaw. Numbers of people were going up from Dolgelly, Towyn, and Barmouth, or rather Arthog, which is three miles nearer. The summit and most of the rocks on the way are, or were, strewn with paper, corks, broken bottles, and such remains. There are no ferns, no flowers, no minerals, nothing but grey stones and tussocky grey grass. Of the view we are not qualified to give an opinion, but Cader himself we voted a barren, untidy mountain.

Coming down, we rested and lunched at a little spring half a mile from the top. It was the only one we had seen, Cader being singularly dry. This struck us very much, as we had been used to bogs for so long that climbing on firm dry ground was quite exhausting.

After lunch, and *à propos* of buns, Margery told the following college story. An Oxford man always made a practice of reading at breakfast. One morning, being immersed in his book, he mechanically cut his roll in two, buttered and eat one half, and was proceeding with the other, when a casual glance revealed six little legs embedded in it! Is the mental picture formed by a geologist, at sight of a single bone of some antediluvian monster, as vivid as was that undergraduate's vision of a cockroach?

Soon it was necessary to start again, so we took a track west for Arthog. We obtained vague directions from a boy guide, but had mostly to depend on our own wits.

The Mawddach estuary and its bridge were below us, but that side of the mountain is very steep, so we went on and up over the turf, which presently improved all along the ridge, till the track ended on the side of Tyrau Mawr, a peak nearly as high as Cader, but turfy all over. After mounting this, we came almost suddenly to the edge, looking right down some two thousand feet to the estuary, with Barmouth in the distance.

After a long rest on the soft dry turf, we began to descend towards the old Towyn road below us. One of the party does not like going downhill, so she packed herself together and tobogganed most of the way, to the ill-concealed merriment of the others.

After following the old grass-grown and deserted road, some children directed us to a path between and over the low hills which skirt the estuary, to the regular path down Cader to Arthog.

Before trudging on to Barmouth, we had a most excellent tea at small cost, in the garden of Clan-y-wern House. The flowers were lovely, especially some splendid begonias.

Some other occupants of the garden afforded us a

good deal of amusement. One lady, grey-haired, with two funny little tight curls depending from a knob behind, wore one of the small tweed fore-and-aft caps affected by so many tourists. It was apparently too big, for every now and then it slipped right over her face, without in the least interrupting her conversation.

Constance was irresistibly reminded of an imperturbable friend, who once fell backward down a short flight of stone steps while talking to a group of ladies. They sprang to his assistance, but he quietly rose, talking all the time, and wished them good afternoon, without even a smile.

Our little grey lady was soon joined by a bandy-legged little man with a long beard and a white straw hat. They made a curious pair, once seen, not easily forgotten.

Leaving Clan-y-wern, after a chat with the kindly hostess, we were directed to follow the railway line to Barmouth. It seems a very common practice hereabouts for people to do this. One train passed us; it was curious to be so near. The line traverses some waste ground, partly bog, partly sand, partly ditch, and wholly beautiful with wild flowers, among which were the yellow iris, bulrushes, meadow-sweet, loose-strife, red, white, and sea-campions, hemp agrimony, vetches, ling, hawkweeds, ragwort, and many others, which made a beautiful foreground to the solemn mountains beyond. From the long bridge which spans the estuary we had a splendid view both ways—westwards, the setting sun, red and glowing; eastwards, the estuary narrowing between ranges of hills and peaks of all tints of purple.

After much difficulty we found quarters at a "Temperance," and hoped to be able to stay over Sunday.

CHAPTER XV.

BARMOUTH TO LLANUWCHYLLYN.

Saturday, August 18.—Owing to the crowded state of Barmouth, which was full to overflowing with "tourist" in its most aggravated form, we had been unable to find very roomy quarters; indeed, Margery and Constance were obliged to put up for the night in another house at some little distance from the one where Leonora and Christina were located. When we met on Saturday morning, it was found that they had not "travelled farther and fared worse," but, on the other hand, considerably better than Leonora and Christina, whose slumbers had been entirely put to flight by a dog whose howls filled the air till dawn, when the numerous cocks of the neighbourhood took up the strain. "Were no other rooms available?" was the first question we asked of our obliging landlady in the morning. She could do nothing else for us, so, as we did not feel sufficiently enamoured of Barmouth in its August aspect to stay till Monday, there was nothing for it but to make up our packs and our minds to go further on.

We took the train to Penmaenpool, as Llanuwchyllyn, where we hoped to put up for Sunday, was beyond our walking powers. At Penmaenpool we stayed an hour or two, Christina being rather tired. Margery walked on to Dolgelly meantime, and joined us in the train there for Drwsynant, where we started again to walk to Llanuwchyllyn, about six and a quarter miles. The road was good, and the walk would have been delightful had it not been for the midges, which were troublesome enough as we walked along, but when we sat down on a wall under some trees to make our tea and rest a while, they were positively unbearable. The road seems not to be much used now, and fortunately there were no passers-by; such would have seen us all pacing up and down, and trying to eat and drink while so doing. There is a slight slope upwards until Bala Lake, or Llyn Tegid, comes in sight, when one is 750 feet above sea-level. After a good view of the lake, we descended again towards the village of Llanuwchyllyn, leaving Cader Idris towering behind us, filling up the end of the valley, and coming in sight of the Arrenigs to the left, and looking down over the lake.

We had met two or three haymakers in knee breeches and stout grey stockings on the way from

Drwsynant, but no tourists, except two ladies, who, we saw in the distance with some amusement, were evidently on an expedition like our own, but in the opposite direction. When we came nearer, Leonora surprised the rest of us by going up to them and having a friendly talk. When she rejoined us, we found they were old fellow-students of hers, who had just come from Llanuwchyllyn, and recommended the hotel there as most comfortable.

When we reached the village we made for the post-office, passing the church, two chapels, and two schools, the National and British. It was then about 7 p.m., and we were rather taken aback to hear that the only rooms in the place were at the hotel or at the national schoolmaster's house. The hotel, a charmingly picturesque one, with an unpronounceable Welsh name, we inspected first, and, though reasonable as hotels go, the terms were beyond our purses at that stage of our tour, as we had firmly resolved not to spend more than £4 10s. each, if it could possibly be avoided. So we had to retrace our steps to the schoolmaster's house, where, after a good deal of indecision and hesitation, we at last obtained three most comfortable rooms, the sitting-room having two luxurious couches, on which Christina and Leonora reposed at the earliest opportunity.

We saw no more of the village that night, as it was

getting late, and we were all glad to rest. One thing that struck us a good deal was the extreme Welshness of everything; indeed, less English seemed to be spoken than in many places much further from the border. We were even told that as a rule there were but three or four English services in the church in the course of the year, when Sir Watkin Williams Wynn comes down to Glanllyn, his house near the lake, for shooting or fishing. Fortunately for us, he had just arrived with his party a day or two before, and there was to be an English service the next afternoon.

CHAPTER XVI.

LLANUWCHYLLYN.

Sunday, August 19.—So far we had none of us been to a Welsh service, and we made up our minds to take this, our last opportunity, and set forth at ten o'clock to the pretty little church.

The congregation was small, but included a very large proportion of men, who, led by the particularly sweet-toned organ, sang most lustily and well. The vicar thoughtfully announced the Psalms, lessons, and hymns, and read the text in English as well as Welsh, for our benefit and that of two other strangers who were present, so that we were able to follow the service with comparative ease.

In the afternoon, our landlord, who seemed to unite the offices of schoolmaster, choirmaster, and organist, and was anxious that the music should go well, persuaded one of the two visitors whom we had seen that morning to play the organ, and himself led the choir, which, as far as we could see, consisted of but two men. The congregation was larger than before, and the singing of the melodious Welsh voices was in itself a treat. The vicar preached a thoughtful and interesting sermon, making a quaint little allusion to an old effigy in the chancel, a knight in armour.

Afterwards Leonora went in to the house, and the others strolled up the road, where they were soon overtaken by the vicar, who told them a good deal about the parish. It must be a somewhat dull position, for few but anglers visit it, and for weeks and weeks in winter it is almost cut off from communication with the surrounding villages, owing to the deep snow. Most of the farms are held by tenant-farmers, who go in for dairying more than anything else. Indeed, *hay* is the most important crop there. Even at this late date, not half of the hay had been got in, and when Sir Watkin started to shoot on the Saturday, he could get none of the men to go with him as beaters, as they were all hard at work in the hayfields.

CHAPTER XVII.

LLANUWCHYLLYN TO CORWEN.

Seventeenth day—Monday, August 20.—The day opened badly with a disagreeable surprise in the shape of a heavier bill than we had anticipated. We had certainly been very comfortable, and the sum total did not *sound* exorbitant, but our previous experiences had led us to expect a less serious demand on our purse, and the figure aroused a desire to quote Mr. Mantalini. From this we refrained, and a courteous but firm remonstrance from Margery, and a reminder that we had expressed a wish not to board by the day, obtained an abatement; but even then our resources were heavily taxed, and, after holding a council of war, we reluctantly decided that our funds would not cover more than one day's expenses and our fare to Birmingham.

We resolved to push on to Corwen (a distance of eighteen miles and a half), and see what we could of the neighbourhood the next morning, giving up all idea of walking through the famous Vale of Llangollen. We had fine weather and a good road all along Bala lake, which was grey but pretty, though more of a lowland lake than the others we had seen.

Bala itself looks rather English. We did not explore the town, only stopping long enough at the post-office to notify our change of plans to our friends. We replenished our provision-bag and trudged on. For the first three miles we kept to the left of the Dee, whose head-waters we crossed near Llanuwchyllyn, and lunched beside it, under some fine beeches, which provided welcome shelter when the rain came on a little later. How placid and innocent, not to say sluggish, the water seemed, and what a remarkably vivid impression it was destined to leave on our minds! For presently this happened. Leonora, true to her instinct of comfort when possible, had spread herself out on a specially attractive bit of turf near the river, with her knapsack arranged as a pillow. This was all very well so long as there was no temptation to stir, but when this temptation presented itself in the shape of a biscuit just out of reach, an incautious movement upset the balance of the knapsack, and before Leonora realized her danger, her worldly goods were in the embrace of the river. Desperation lent her a swiftness which fortunately the

Dee did not possess, and while the others waited to laugh, she went to the rescue, and successfully landed the knapsack, damp and draggled.

Mr. Mantalini was for a second time the exponent of our feelings. However, when we examined the extent of the damage we found that very little harm was done, and after all the dampness was only a foretaste of what was to prevail later in the day.

We waited under the trees until they ceased to afford much protection from the rain, solacing ourselves with some extremely light literature; but when it became necessary to put up umbrellas, we thought it was time to move on in search of a more permanent shelter.

If our conscience would permit us to suppress facts, we would gladly draw a veil over the events of the next few hours, but we have promised a "plain unvarnished tale," and the rough as well as the smooth must be set down here.

Before making a start, we found ourselves face to face with the long-deferred question of adjusting a mackintosh cloak *and* a knapsack.

Under the dripping beech trees we worked out the problem, and found that it admitted of at least four solutions. Margery's was the speediest and certainly the neatest, for her woollen cloak was made with a half-cape, which enabled her to arrange the straps with tolerable (*only* tolerable!) comfort, and balance the pack under her arm.

The other three cloaks were of the old-fashioned round shape, with slits instead of sleeves, and any reader who tries to strap on a knapsack *over* such a garment will readily understand that we were baffled in our attempts to combine comfort with any degree of elegance, even the minimum.

Christina fashioned her cloak into a skirt, wore her pack as usual, and trusted to her umbrella for further shelter.

Constance, after many ingenious efforts, adopted the simple expedient of linking the two straps, passing them round her neck, and holding them with one hand, her pack resting as usual.

Leonora, for some reason best known to herself, insisted on sheltering her already damp pack, and wore the cloak *over* it, thereby producing an effect which required to be seen to be appreciated.

Our line of route lay through a peaceful, and doubtless, on a sunny day, a pretty, smiling land, but we noticed with a feeling of regret that at every step the country grew more and more English, and even the rippling waters of the Dee did not compensate for the wilder beauty of the streams we had left behind. It is needful to remark, however, that during the latter part of this day's walk the scenery made but slight impression upon us.

We are pledged to be veracious, but we are not called upon to dilate on our miseries. More than once in the course of this narrative have we checked the outpourings of enthusiasm, lest we weary our friends, and by so doing we hope we have earned the right to shorten the road from Bala to Corwen.

The rain rained steadily, relentlessly, and we walked—not so steadily, for we grew very wet and very weary, and in the words of the poet—

"The soul, mistrusting, asks if this be joy."

We reached Corwen at six o'clock, our philosophy and our legs about equally exhausted, the soft muddy roads having been a great hindrance to our progress; but even in that supreme moment of fatigue and discomfort, we were agreed that we had had enough enjoyment in the past sixteen days to make up for a dozen more such walks, if need be.

And here we may introduce a subject we have only touched upon before, namely, the almost unfailing kindliness and thoughtfulness of the various hostesses whose roofs had sheltered us. At Ogwen, at Penrhyn, Dolgelly, and other places, we had been cared for, and sent on our way with many pleasant words, and here at Corwen nothing could exceed the attentions of good Mrs. Davies and her daughter, to whose house we were directed by a most obliging post-office official. Mrs. Davies received us—evidently fresh from the wash-tub—brought us at once into her bright, warm, clean houseplace, ordered her small son Llewellyn out of the way, and proceeded to dry, warm, feed and clothe four dripping mortals, who descended thus upon her as if from the skies—and, as we found next day, without any after-thought of extra remuneration. Wales and the Welsh (*women*, at any rate) have risen many degrees in our esteem.

One thing, however, was needed, and that was supper, or rather its materials, for, taught by experience, we usually marketed for ourselves, if possible. Margery, as being the least exhausted, foraged through the little town, and after surviving several interminable Welsh conversations in the shops grouped round the little market-place, returned with delicious brown and white bread and butter; but the whole town could not provide more than six eggs, to be divided between four. As Mrs. Davies seemed to have no solution to the problem, Margery, already the cook of the party as far as "billy-tea" was concerned, begged the loan of some kitchen utensils, and soon produced a dish of buttered eggs, our hostess looking on with interest the while.

CHAPTER XVIII.

CORWEN TO BIRMINGHAM.

Tuesday, August 21.—Before setting out to investigate the various objects of interest in Corwen, we were much amused at the sight on which our sitting-room window looked down. Corwen is a regular country market-town, and quite early the streets were thronged with farmers and country folk, bringing their produce—mostly pigs—for sale, and who took up their station in the main street. The antics of the pigs were most laughable; one poor old woman in particular excited our pity. She was driving two pigs in a leash, and when pig number one made up his mind to go north, pig number two was pretty sure to have determined to go south, and so on.

We had to wait some little time for our boots, whose soaking on Monday had proved too much for them; but, after careful oiling, etc., by our most considerate landlady, we managed to get them on, and, all but Leonora started for the church, parts of which are extremely old, dating back, according to tradition, to long before Owain Glyndwr's time. In the churchyard we noticed an old armless inscribed cross, interesting to the antiquary for its markings, which correspond with those found on cromlechs and other ancient stones. In a stone which now forms the lintel of the priest's door, we saw a rude cross, lying horizontally, and looking to us as if the stone had simply been wrongly placed; this, however, is famous as the supposed true mark of Owain Glyndwr's dagger, when he threw it from the hills overlooking the village. Owain is the prevailing hero of the neighbourhood, and everything in the least inexplicable is at once put down to him.

Many of the older graves have "kneeling-stones," where it is believed people used to come and pray for the departed. These are low head and foot stones, shaped thus:

We found every gradation from this shape to the more modern—

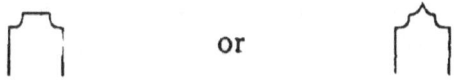

and as the oldest tombs with the kneeling-stones appear from the dates to be no older than 1750, it seems probable that the *form* has been kept, while the purpose which they served has been lost.

Inside the church is a very old tomb and effigy of a priest (Iorwerth Sulien), holding the chalice in his hands. It is in a low recess in the north wall of the chancel.

By the time we left the church it was raining slightly, and we went back to our rooms to consult with Leonora as to our future movements. We had hoped to walk on to Llangollen, and thence take the train homewards, but *experientia docet*. The sky looked so threatening that we were afraid to risk another such walk as that from Bala to Corwen, and we, therefore, reluctantly decided on the next through train for Birmingham. There was an hour or so to spare before that was due, and so we set out to see a splendid view from the "flagstaff," which stands on a high cairn (erected in commemoration of the Prince of Wales' wedding), on a peak directly overlooking the town, the spot whence Glyndwr is said to have thrown his dagger. The rain came on rather heavily as we reached the top, and obscured the distant view, where Snowdon is visible on a clear day, but we got a good idea of the town, and had a last look at the silver Dee, and Telford's Holyhead Road winding away north-west to Bettws-y-Coed.

We made our way down the hill, picked up Leonora

and our packs at our lodgings, and with considerable difficulty pressed through the throngs of beasts and men to the station, where we secured a through carriage, and were soon whirling past Llangollen on to Ruabon, where the train turned south towards Birmingham. It was difficult to judge of Llangollen from the railway line, and on such a showery day, but we were not so much impressed with it as we expected. Certainly the best way to see the vale is to take it in the opposite direction, and walk seawards.

There was not much of interest to describe on the homeward journey. Near Ruabon we crossed part of the Denbighshire coal-field, and saw the grim chimneys and slag-heaps and winding-gear disfiguring the pretty wooded and heathy district. The appearance of lime-kilns, too, near Llangollen, warned us that we had left the slates behind, and had passed into the limestone region.

As we neared our destination, Christina caused some amusement by bringing out the remains of the store of chocolate, and making us all finish it, so that she might receive praise for her good management in having provided just enough for the tour.

Birmingham greeted us with a thunderstorm, and though we were all sad to think that our delightful holiday was at an end, it was some consolation to feel that we had not to begin a search for a shelter for the night.

CHAPTER XIX.

SUPPLEMENTARY.

At the end of this account of our decidedly successful tramp through North Wales, it may not be out of place to mention some of the conclusions to which we have come, and the experience we have gained.

1. We have all improved in health, and three of our number have increased in weight.

2. We have come home with our geographical knowledge widened, and our minds stored with memories of beautiful scenery.

3. We have had a seventeen days' holiday for less than £4 10s. each, and withal have done nothing that people in ordinary health, with sufficient common sense, a small bump of locality, a good map, and their "weather-eye" open, cannot easily accomplish, even in doubtful weather; for it is the opinion of some at least of our party that Wales looks best in a rainy season, if it does not rain every day.

The *distances* done by us were as a rule very moderate. The following list may be interesting:—

1st day	6 miles.		
2nd ,,	11 ,,		
3rd ,,	13 ,,		
4th ,,	12 ,,		
5th ,,	7½ ,,	With hard climbing.	
6th ,,	6 ,,		
7th ,,	13½ ,,	8 in rain.	
8th ,,	6 ,,		
9th ,,	9 ,,	including Moel Hebog.	
10th ,,	16 ,,	including Snowdon.	
11th ,,	21 ,,	6 too many.	
12th ,,	6 ,,		
13th ,,	17 ,,	including Cader Idris.	
14th ,,	8 ,,		
15th ,,	2 ,,		
16th ,,	18½ ,,	9½ in steady rain and *mud*.	
17th ,,	2 ,,		

making a total of 174½ miles

We have given all the distances actually walked, though it will be seen that on Sundays and other rest-days, they consisted rather of short strolls than real walks.

An *analysis* of our expenditure may also be of use.

	£	s.	d.
Railway fares for four (including two short journeys)..	3	16	9½
Lodgings for 17 nights for four	4	15	9
Food for 17 days	7	9	9
Drives and admission to places of interest..	1	7	2½
Miscellaneous expenses		4	0
	£17	13	6

This, divided by four, gives £4 8s. 4½d. as the share of each member of the party. Personal expenses, such as postage and photographs, were, of course, paid for individually.

We provided ourselves with small light knapsacks, and the following articles, which were common property :—

> The Gossiping Guide to North Wales.
> Four sheets of the ordnance map, large size.
> Small ordnance map of North Wales.
> Blotting-paper.
> Ink.
> Envelopes and paper.
> Small " etna."
> Methylated spirits.
> Small tin saucepan.
> Tea.
> Chocolate *menier*.
> Raisins.
> Tin of meat-paste and Liebig.
> Clothes-brush.
> Vaseline.
> Brandy. ⎫ Not used.
> Calendula, aconite, chlorodyne. ⎭
> Small work-case.
> Matches.
> Soap and towel.

We were each responsible for a share of the above, and filled the remaining space in our knapsacks with the articles we severally considered most indispensable.

In conclusion, we wish to offer a few suggestions to any who feel called upon to follow our example.

1. Take nothing unnecessary. Changes of clothing are easily sent and exchanged by parcel-post.
2. Provide yourselves with good chocolate and some raisins, and have recourse to one or other as soon as you feel in the least fatigued.
3. The above, with sandwiches and buns, and tea made by the wayside, will be found sufficient food while actually on the road. Get a good meat meal at the end of the day, with coffee or cocoa.
4. Begin the walking gradually, and do not walk just for the sake of covering the ground.
5. Do not walk onwards on persistently wet days, unless compelled by circumstances.
6. Carry a small towel and piece of soap in an accessible place.
7. Have a small drinking-cup.
8. A deep detachable under-pocket is most useful.
9. We must leave to other travellers the task of discovering a happy solution of the cloak question. Our last word on the subject is, "avoid mackintoshes."

THE END.

www.ingramcontent.com/pod-product-compliance
Lightning Source LLC
Chambersburg PA
CBHW020126170426
43199CB00009B/664